1st EDITION

Perspectives on Diseases and Disorders

Lymphoma

Arthur Gillard
Book Editor

PERSPECTIVES
On Diseases & Disorders

GALE
CENGAGE Learning

Detroit • New York • San Francisco • New Haven, Conn • Waterville, Maine • London

616.944
L986

Elizabeth Des Chenes, *Managing Editor*

LIBRARY OF CONGRESS CATALOGING-IN-PUBLICATION DATA

Lymphoma / Arthur Gillard, book editor.
    p. cm. -- (Perspectives on diseases and disorders)
  Includes bibliographical references and index.
  ISBN 978-0-7377-5778-1 (hardback)
  1. Lymphomas--Popular works. I. Gillard, Arthur.
  RC280.L9L9523 2012
  616.99'446--dc23

                                                        2011053376

CONTENTS

Rosalyn Carson-DeWitt and Margaret Alic

Hodgkin's lymphoma, also known as Hodgkin's disease, is a cancer that originates in the lymphatic system. It occurs most commonly in people aged 15 to 40 or over 55. The cause of Hodgkin's is unknown but may be a combination of genetics, environmental exposures, and infectious agents. Current treatments are highly effective.

Lata Cherath

At least ten different types of non-Hodgkin's lymphoma exist, grouped according to how vigorously they grow and how far they spread. Most of these lymphomas start in the lymph nodes, although about one in five start in other organs. More males are affected than females, and risk increases with age.

LymphomaInfo.net

Various factors are known to increase the risk of developing lymphoma, including environmental factors such as exposure to certain chemicals, as well as immune system disorders and certain infectious agents.

FOREWORD

"Medicine, to produce health, has to examine disease."
—Plutarch

Independent research on a health issue is often the first step to complement discussions with a physician. But locating accurate, well-organized, understandable medical information can be a challenge. A simple Internet search on terms such as "cancer" or "diabetes," for example, returns an intimidating number of results. Sifting through the results can be daunting, particularly when some of the information is inconsistent or even contradictory. The Greenhaven Press series Perspectives on Diseases and Disorders offers a solution to the often overwhelming nature of researching diseases and disorders.

From the clinical to the personal, titles in the Perspectives on Diseases and Disorders series provide students and other researchers with authoritative, accessible information in unique anthologies that include basic information about the disease or disorder, controversial aspects of diagnosis and treatment, and first-person accounts of those impacted by the disease. The result is a well-rounded combination of primary and secondary sources that, together, provide the reader with a better understanding of the disease or disorder.

Each volume in Perspectives on Diseases and Disorders explores a particular disease or disorder in detail. Material for each volume is carefully selected from a wide range of sources, including encyclopedias, journals, newspapers, nonfiction books, speeches, government documents, pamphlets, organization newsletters, and position papers. Articles in the first chapter provide an authoritative, up-to-date overview that covers symptoms, causes and effects, treatments, cures, and medical advances. The second chapter presents a substantial number of opposing viewpoints on controversial treatments and other current debates relating to the volume topic. The third chapter offers a variety of personal perspectives on the disease or disorder. Patients, doctors, caregivers, and loved ones represent just some of the voices found in this narrative chapter.

Each Perspectives on Diseases and Disorders volume also includes:

- An **annotated table of contents** that provides a brief summary of each article in the volume.

- An **introduction** specific to the volume topic.

- Full-color **charts and graphs** to illustrate key points, concepts, and theories.

- Full-color **photos** that show aspects of the disease or disorder and enhance textual material.

- **"Fast Facts"** that highlight pertinent additional statistics and surprising points.

- A **glossary** providing users with definitions of important terms.

- A **chronology** of important dates relating to the disease or disorder.

- An annotated list of **organizations to contact** for students and other readers seeking additional information.

- A **bibliography** of additional books and periodicals for further research.

- A detailed **subject index** that allows readers to quickly find the information they need.

Whether a student researching a disorder, a patient recently diagnosed with a disease, or an individual who simply wants to learn more about a particular disease or disorder, a reader who turns to Perspectives on Diseases and Disorders will find a wealth of information in each volume that offers not only basic information, but also vigorous debate from multiple perspectives.

INTRODUCTION

Lymphoma is a group of disorders that arise from abnormalities in the development of lymphocytes, disease-fighting white blood cells that originate in the bone marrow. Because there are a number of different lymphocytes, and different stages of development for each one, lymphoma can show up in many different ways. Over the years a variety of increasingly sophisticated classification systems have been developed to accurately describe the many different forms of lymphoma, with the World Health Organization (WHO) classification developed in 2001 and revised in 2008 being considered the currently authoritative standard for describing lymphoma.

Lymphoma is a blood cancer, the most common type of blood cancer in the United States. (The other varieties of blood cancer are leukemia and myeloma.) Blood cancers develop from abnormalities in any of the stages of development of blood cells—not just the lymphocytes or white blood cells but also platelets, red blood cells, and so on. There is some categorical overlap between leukemia and lymphoma—which illustrates the complexity of lymphoma in particular and blood cancers in general—so that in some cases essentially the same disease process can be considered either a lymphoma or leukemia, depending on how it manifests in the body at the time that it is discovered.

The most striking example of this involves the diseases chronic lymphocytic leukemia (CLL) and small lymphocytic lymphoma (SLL). CLL shows up as cancer cells circulating in the blood and is the most common type of leukemia. SLL shows up as cancer cells in the lymph nodes and is a type of non-Hodgkin's lymphoma (NHL), accounting for about 4 to 5 percent of cases of NHL each year. Both start out as an excess growth of the same type of white blood cells in the bone marrow and will be diagnosed as lymphoma or leukemia depending on where they are most prevalent (lymph nodes or blood) at the time of diagnosis.

In the literature on lymphoma one will often encounter the terms "Hodgkin's lymphoma" (sometimes referred to as "Hodgkin's disease") and "non-Hodgkin's lymphoma." Hodgkin's was the first type of lymphoma to be clearly identified, in a paper published in 1832 by English pathologist Thomas Hodgkin. It is a relatively simple and—these days—usually easy to treat form of lymphoma, with a high cure rate.

Hodgkin's lymphoma originates with B cells, one of the main types of lymphocytes, and is characterized by a distinctive type of cell known as Reed-Sternberg cells. These cells are quite large and contain more than one nucleus (cells normally have only one). It is most prevalent in people in their teens and early twenties, as well as those in their fifties.

Non-Hodgkin's lymphoma does not have Reed-Sternberg cells. NHL most commonly arises from B cells, and sometimes from T cells. Whereas HL has only a few ways of manifesting, NHL comes in a bewildering variety of forms. Non-Hodgkin's lymphoma can strike at any age but generally increases in incidence as people get older.

Most often the "presenting symptom" for lymphoma, that is, the symptom that prompts people to visit their doctor for a diagnosis, is enlarged or swollen lymph glands, usually in the neck, armpit, or groin—areas where it is possible to feel the swellings. Usually the lumps are painless unless the lymphoma is aggressive and the swelling has grown rapidly.

In other cases, the disease progresses in ways that are not noticeable until the lymphoma is quite advanced, as in Steve Collins's case. In a February 27, 2011, *Sunday Times* (London) article, his daughter Amy Malloy reports:

> Our family's ordeal began in July 2004. I was away at university when I got the call to come to the hospital. My mother's voice was flat, stunned. When my father [Steve Collins] had gone to bed the night before, everything had seemed normal. But he had woken up paralyzed from the waist down. In hindsight, the cancer, non-Hodgkin's lymphoma [NHL], had been causing symptoms for six months. Tiredness, weight loss, a slight shortness of breath—but he had put it down to stress.

For Collins, after starting in his lymph nodes the disease spread through his bloodstream, forming a tumor around his spine that eventually put pressure on his nerves and caused the paralysis that was his presenting symptom.

Doctors now have a wide variety of treatment modalities available to treat lymphoma, with more being developed all the time. This is an exciting time for lymphoma research, with new scientific discoveries and technologies becoming available, improving the outlook for people with lymphoma. (Consider that the survival rate for Hodgkin's lymphoma increased from about 40 percent in 1960 to 88 percent in 2006; for non-Hodgkin's lymphoma, comparable figures are 31 percent in 1960 and 69.1 percent in 2006.)

Chemotherapy and/or radiation therapy are typical treatments for lymphoma, but in Collins's case his lymphoma was already so advanced the only option that gave him a fighting chance was a stem cell transplant, a more radical and risky treatment with extremely debilitating and unpleasant side-effects and a high chance of death. But faced with the alternative of certainly dying from his lymphoma in the near future, it is not surprising that Steve—along with fifty thousand other cancer patients each year in the United States—opted for the stem cell treatment.

Thomas Hodgkin identified the first type of lymphoma in 1832. Today, this form of lymphoma is treatable and has a high cure rate. (© SPL/Photo Researchers, Inc.)

Stem cells are undifferentiated cells found in bone marrow and other tissues that can potentially mature into many different types of cells, helping the body to replenish and repair itself. Blood stem cells produce all of the different types of blood cells. In the type of stem cell transplant used to treat lymphoma, cells are either taken from a compatible donor or—as in Collins's case—harvested from the patient's own blood. The patient is then given very high doses of chemotherapy to eradicate all the body's cancer cells, but the doses are so high that the bone marrow is destroyed as well, meaning the patient can no longer produce enough blood cells on his or her own. Finally, the stem cells that were previously harvested are put back into the bloodstream intravenously. During that phase the patient is kept in strict isolation until the stem cells are able to replenish the immune system, because until they do the smallest infection could be fatal.

Steve was in isolation for more than a month, during which he suffered side effects such as night sweats, vomiting, and diarrhea. He insists that the ordeal was harder on those caring for him than for himself, saying, "I was so heavily drugged it felt like a dream. I didn't have the strength to worry or wonder 'what if . . . ?' As the patient you become quite selfish—there were days when I'd lie there and not want anyone near me." His wife was the only one allowed into his room to see him (after using appropriate sterilization procedures). She had to feed him with a spoon and he would not talk or look at her. She reports that, "It was a very lonely time. His mind was in another place. He wouldn't communicate hello or goodbye. It was like having a baby under the covers."

Steve gradually recovered from the difficult treatment, although it was a year before he could go a week without throwing up, and it took two full years before he felt in control of his body again. Asked if he felt it was worth going through the treatment, he responded, "Of course. I was young and had a family to live for." Although his treatment journey was a harrowing one, he's been in remission for six years.

In *Perspectives on Diseases and Disorders: Lymphoma* the contributing authors discuss and debate the causes of, treatments for, and controversies surrounding lymphoma, and relate personal experiences of suffering from this disease.

CHAPTER 1

Understanding Lymphoma

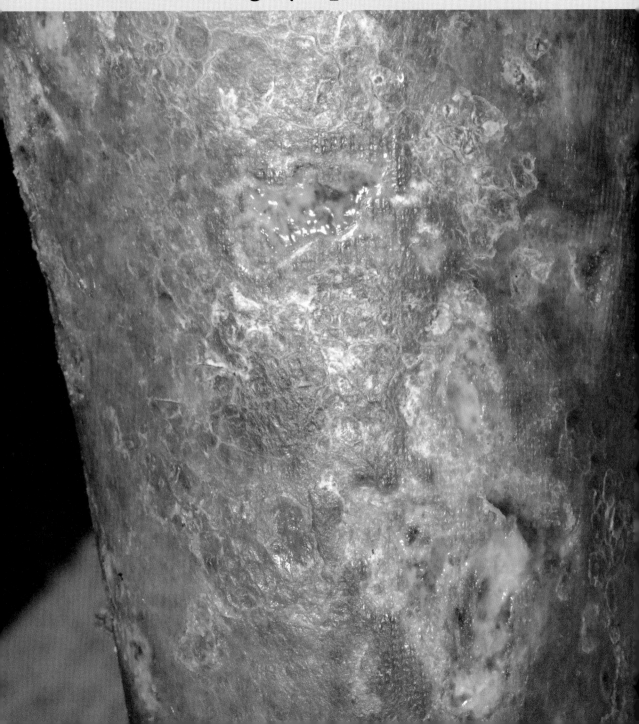

Hodgkin's Lymphoma

Rosalyn Carson-DeWitt and Margaret Alic

Rosalyn Carson-DeWitt has written and edited hundreds of medical articles for print, Internet, and CD-ROM products and is the editor-in-chief of *Drugs, Alcohol, and Tobacco: Learning About Drugs, Alcohol, and Addictive Behavior.* Margaret Alic is a science writer, a researcher in molecular biology at the Oregon Graduate Center, and author of *Hypatia's Heritage: A History of Women in Science from Antiquity to the Late Nineteenth Century.*

In the following viewpoint Carson-DeWitt and Alic describe Hodgkin's disease (also known as Hodgkin's lymphoma), a highly curable form of lymphoma discovered by a British physician named Thomas Hodgkin in 1832. The authors describe the characteristics and symptoms of the disease, as well as its stages and treatments. According to the authors, between 85 percent and 95 percent of people diagnosed with Hodgkin's disease will be alive five years after diagnosis.

Photo on previous page. Pictured here are mycosis fungoides ulcers on an eighty-three-year-old man. Mycosis fungoides is a rare non-Hodgkin's cancer of the lymphoid tissue affecting primarily the skin. (© Dr. P. Marazzi/Photo Researchers, Inc.)

SOURCE: Rosalyn Carson-DeWitt and Margaret Alic, *Gale Encyclopedia of Medicine,* 3rd edition. Belmont, CA: The Gale Group, 2006, pp. 1818. Copyright © 2006 by The Gale Group. All rights reserved. Reproduced by permission.

Hodgkin's disease is a rare lymphoma, a cancer of the lymphatic system.

Hodgkin's disease, or Hodgkin's lymphoma, was first described in 1832 by Thomas Hodgkin, a British physician. Hodgkin clearly differentiated between this disease and the much more common non-Hodgkin's lymphomas. Prior to 1970, few individuals survived Hodgkin's disease. Now, however, the majority of individuals with this cancer can be cured.

The lymphatic system is part of the body's immune system, for fighting disease, and a part of the blood-producing system. It includes the lymph vessels and nodes, and the spleen, bone marrow, and thymus. The narrow lymphatic vessels carry lymphatic fluid from throughout the body. The lymph nodes are small organs that filter the lymphatic fluid and trap foreign substances, including viruses, bacteria, and cancer cells. The spleen, in the upper left abdomen, removes old cells and debris from the blood. The bone marrow, the tissue inside the bones, produces new red and white blood cells.

Lymphocytes are white blood cells that recognize and destroy disease-causing organisms. Lymphocytes are produced in the lymph nodes, spleen, and bone marrow. They circulate throughout the body in the blood and lymphatic fluid. Clusters of immune cells also exist in major organs.

Characteristics of Hodgkin's Disease

Hodgkin's disease is a type of lymphoma in which antibody-producing cells of the lymphatic system begin to grow abnormally. It usually begins in a lymph node and progresses slowly, in a fairly predictable way, spreading via the lymphatic vessels from one group of lymph nodes to the next. Sometimes it invades organs that are adjacent to the lymph nodes. If the cancer cells spread to the blood, the disease can reach almost any site in the body. Advanced cases of Hodgkin's disease may involve the spleen, liver, bone marrow, and lungs.

There are different subtypes of Hodgkin's disease:

- nodular sclerosis (30–60% of cases)
- mixed cellularity (20–40 % of cases)
- lymphocyte predominant (5–10% of cases)
- lymphocyte depleted (less than 5% of cases)
- unclassified . . .

Hodgkin's disease can occur at any age. However, the majority of cases develop in early adulthood (ages 15–40) and late adulthood (after age 55). Approximately 10–15% of cases are in children under age 17. It is more common in boys than in girls under the age of 10. The disease is very rare in children under five.

Symptoms of Hodgkin's Disease

The cause of Hodgkin's disease is not known. It is suspected that some interaction between an individual's genetic makeup, environmental exposures, and infectious agents may be responsible. Immune system deficiencies also may be involved.

Early symptoms of Hodgkin's disease may be similar to those of the flu:

- fevers, night sweats, chills
- fatigue
- loss of appetite
- weight loss
- itching
- pain after drinking alcoholic beverages
- swelling of one or more lymph nodes

Sudden or emergency symptoms of Hodgkin's disease include:

- sudden high fever
- loss of bladder and/or bowel control
- numbness in the arms and legs and a loss of strength

As lymph nodes swell, they may push on other structures, causing a variety of symptoms:

- pain due to pressure on nerve roots
- loss of function in muscle groups served by compressed nerves
- coughing or shortness of breath due to compression of the windpipe and/or airways, by swollen lymph nodes in the chest
- kidney failure from compression of the ureters, the tubes that carry urine from the kidneys to the bladder
- swelling in the face, neck, or legs, due to pressure on veins
- paralysis in the legs due to pressure on the spinal cord

As Hodgkin's disease progresses, the immune system becomes less effective at fighting infection. Thus, patients with Hodgkin's lymphoma become more susceptible to both common infections caused by bacteria and unusual (opportunistic) infections. Later symptoms of Hodgkin's disease include the formation of tumors.

Significantly, as many as 75% of individuals with Hodgkin's disease do not have any typical symptoms.

Diagnosis of Hodgkin's Disease

As with many forms of cancer, diagnosis of Hodgkin's disease has two major components.

- identification of Hodgkin's lymphoma as the cause of the patient's disease
- staging of the disease to determine how far the cancer has spread

The initial diagnosis of Hodgkin's disease often results from abnormalities in a chest x ray that was performed because of nonspecific symptoms. The physician then takes a medical history to check for the presence of symptoms and conducts a complete physical examination.

Lymphatic System

The lymphatic system (which includes the spleen) is comprised of a vast network of glands or nodes essential to the immune system.

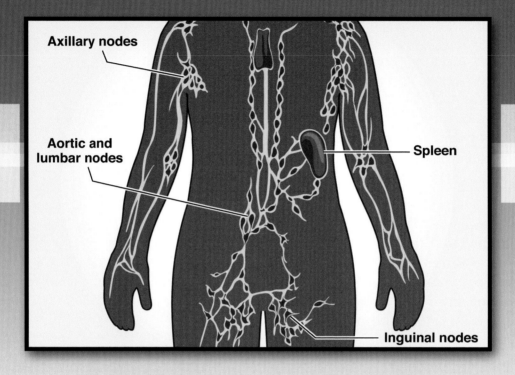

Taken from: "Lymphoma, Hodgkin's Disease." John's Hopkins Symptoms and Remedies, 2008. http://hopkins.portfolio.crushlovely.com.

The size, tenderness, firmness, and location of swollen lymph nodes are determined and correlated with any signs of infection. In particular, lymph nodes that do not shrink after treatment with antibiotics may be a cause for concern. The lymph nodes that are most often affected by Hodgkin's disease include those of the neck, above the collarbone, under the arms, and in the chest above the diaphragm.

Diagnosis of Hodgkin's disease requires either the removal of an entire enlarged lymph node (an excisional

PERSPECTIVES ON DISEASES AND DISORDERS

biopsy) or an incisional biopsy, in which only a small part of a large tumor is removed. If the node is near the skin, the biopsy is performed with a local anesthetic. However, if it is inside the chest or abdomen, general anesthesia is required.

The sample of biopsied tissue is examined under a microscope. Giant cells called Reed-Sternberg cells must be present to confirm a diagnosis of Hodgkin's disease. These cells, which usually contain two or more nuclei, are named for the two pathologists who discovered them. Normal cells have only one nucleus (the organelle within the cell that contains the genetic material). Affected lymph nodes may contain only a few Reed-Sternberg cells and they may be difficult to recognize. Characteristics of other types of cells in the biopsied tissue help to diagnose the subtype of Hodgkin's disease. . . .

Stages of Hodgkin's Disease

Staging is very important in Hodgkin's disease. This is because the cancer usually spreads in a predictable pattern, without skipping sets of lymph nodes until late in the progression of the disease.

Imaging of the abdomen, chest, and pelvis is used to identify areas of enlarged lymph nodes and abnormalities in the spleen or other organs. . . . These images will reveal rounded lumps called nodules in the affected lymph nodes and other organs. . . .

All of the available treatments for Hodgkin's disease have serious side effects, both short and long-term. However, with accurate staging, physicians and patients often can choose the minimum treatment that will cure the disease. The staging system for Hodgkin's disease is the Ann Arbor Staging Classification, also called the Cotswold System or the Revised Ann Arbor System.

FAST FACT

Only about 5 percent of a Hodgkin's lymphoma tumor is made up of cancer cells, with the other 95 percent being various inflamed cells, according to a 2010 *Science Daily* report.

Hodgkin's disease is divided into four stages, with additional substages:

- Stage I: The disease is confined to one lymph node area
- Stage IE: The disease extends from the one lymph node area to adjacent regions
- Stage II: The disease is in two or more lymph node areas on one side of the diaphragm (the muscle below the lungs)
- Stage IIE: The disease extends to adjacent regions of at least one of these nodes
- Stage III: The disease is in lymph node areas on both sides of the diaphragm
- Stage IIIE/IIISE: The disease extends into adjacent areas or organs (IIIE) and/or the spleen (IIISE)
- Stage IV: The disease has spread from the lymphatic system to one or more other organs, such as the bone marrow or liver

Treatment for Hodgkin's disease depends both on the stage of the disease and whether or not symptoms are present. Stages are labeled with an A if no symptoms are present. If symptoms are present, the stage is labeled with a B. These symptoms include:

- loss of more than 10% of body weight over the previous six months
- fevers above 100 (37.70 C) degrees F
- drenching night sweats

Radiation and Chemotherapy

Radiation therapy and/or chemotherapy (drug therapy) are the standard treatments for Hodgkin's disease. If the disease is confined to one area of the body, radiotherapy is usually used. This treatment, with x rays or other high-energy rays, also is used when the disease is in bulky areas such as the chest, where chemotherapeutic drugs cannot reach all of the cancer....

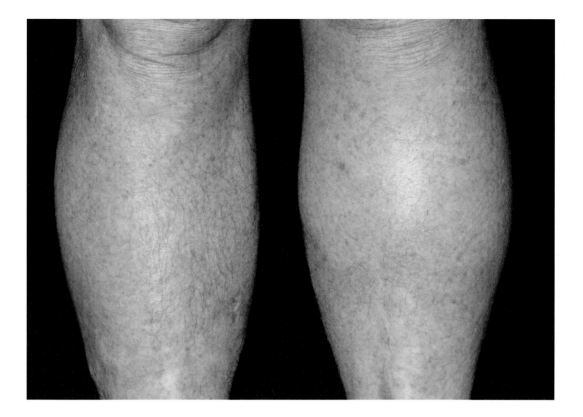

If the Hodgkin's disease has progressed to additional lymph nodes or other organs, or if there is a recurrence of the disease within two years of radiation treatment, chemotherapy is used.

Chemotherapy utilizes a combination of drugs, each of which kills cancer cells in a different way. The most common chemotherapy regimens for Hodgkin's disease are MOPP (either mechlorethamine or methotrexate with Oncovin, procarbazine, prednisone) and ABVD (Adriamycin or doxorubicin, bleomycin, vincristine, dacarbazine). Each of these consists of four different drugs. ABVD is used more frequently than MOPP because it has fewer severe side effects. However MOPP is used for individuals who are at risk for heart failure. The chemotherapeutic drugs may be injected into a vein or muscle, or taken orally, as a pill or liquid. . . .

Hodgkin's disease is a cancer of the lymphatic system that causes swelling due to malfunction of the lymph glands. (© **Dr. P. Marazzi/Photo Researchers, Inc.**)

Other Therapeutic Interventions

An autologous bone marrow and/or a peripheral blood stem cell transplantation (PBSCT) often is recommended for treating resistant or recurrent Hodgkin's disease, particularly if the disease recurs within a few months of a chemotherapy-induced remission. These transplants are autologous because they utilize the individual's own cells. The patient's bone marrow cells or peripheral blood stem cells (immature bone marrow cells found in the blood) are collected and frozen prior to high-dosage chemotherapy, which destroys bone marrow cells. A procedure called leukapheresis is used to collect the stem cells. Following the high-dosage chemotherapy, and possibly radiation, the bone marrow cells or stem cells are reinjected into the individual.

Most complementary therapies for Hodgkin's disease are designed to stimulate the immune system to destroy cancer cells and repair normal cells that have been damaged by treatment. These therapies are used in conjunction with standard treatment.

Immunologic therapies, also known as immunotherapies, biological therapies, or biological response modifier therapies, utilize substances that are produced by the immune system. These include interferon (an immune system protein), monoclonal antibodies (specially engineered antibodies) . . . and vaccines. Many immunotherapies for Hodgkin's disease are experimental and available only through clinical trials. These biological agents may have side effects.

Coenzyme Q10 (CoQ10) and polysaccharide K (PSK) are being evaluated for their ability to stimulate the immune system and protect healthy tissue, as well as possible anti-cancer activities. Camphor, also known as 714-X, green tea, and hoxsey (which is a mixture of a number of substances), have been promoted as immune system enhancers. However, there is no evidence that they are effective against Hodgkin's disease. Hoxsey, in particular, can produce serious side effects.

Hodgkin's disease, particularly in children, is one of the most curable forms of cancer. Approximately 90% of individuals are cured of the disease with chemotherapy and/or radiation.

The one-year relative survival rate following treatment for Hodgkin's disease is 93%. Relative survival rates do not include individuals who die of causes other than Hodgkin's disease. The percentage of individuals who have not died of Hodgkin's disease within five years of diagnosis is 90–95% for those with stage I or stage II disease. The figure is 85–90% for those diagnosed with stage III Hodgkin's and approximately 80% for those diagnosed with stage IV disease. The 15-year relative survival rate is 63%. Approximately 75% of children are alive and cancer free 20 years after the original diagnosis of Hodgkin's.

Non-Hodgkin's Lymphoma

Lata Cherath

Lata Cherath has a PhD in microbiology from the State University of New York Upstate Medical Center in Syracuse and an MD from the New Jersey Medical School.

In the following viewpoint Cherath describes non-Hodgkin's lympoma. According to Cherath, there are at least ten distinct types of non-Hodgkin's lymphomas, which are further divided into stages based on how quickly they grow, as well as how far they spread. Cherath details causes and symptoms and explains how non-Hodgkin's lymphoma is diagnosed. She notes that the survival rate from these lymphomas depends on many factors, such as type of lymphoma and the stage of the disease, as well as the age and general health of the patient.

The lymph system is made up of ducts or tubules that carry lymph to all parts of the body. Lymph is a milky fluid that contains the lymphocytes or white blood cells. These are the infection-fighting cells of the blood. Small pea-shaped organs are found along

SOURCE: Lata Cherath, *Gale Encyclopedia of Medicine,* 3rd edition. Belmont, CA: The Gale Group, 2006, p. 2322. Copyright © 2006 by The Gale Group. All rights reserved. Reproduced by permission.

the network of lymph vessels. These are called the lymph nodes, and their main function is to make and store the lymphocytes. . . .

The lymphocyte is the main cell of the lymphoid tissue. There are two main types of lymphocytes: the T lymphocyte and the B lymphocyte. Lymphomas develop from these two cell types. B cell lymphomas are more common among adults, while among children, the incidence of T and B cell lymphomas are almost equal.

The T and the B cells perform different jobs within the immune system. When an infectious bacterium enters the body, the B cell makes proteins called "antibodies." These antibodies attach themselves to the bacteria, and flag them for destruction by other immune cells. The T cells help protect the body against viruses. When a virus enters the cell, it generally produces certain proteins that are projected on the surface of the infected cell. T cells recognize these proteins and produce certain substances (cytokines) that destroy the infected cells. Some of the cytokines made by the T cells attract other cell types, which are capable of digesting the virus-infected cell. The T cells can also destroy some types of cancerous cells.

Lymphomas can be divided into two main types: Hodgkin's lymphoma or Hodgkin's disease, and non-Hodgkin's lymphomas. There are at least 10 types of non-Hodgkin's lymphomas. They are grouped (staged) by how aggressively they grow; slow growing (low grade), intermediate growing, and rapidly growing (high grade); and how far they spread.

A majority of non-Hodgkin's lymphomas begin in the lymph nodes. About 20% start in other organs, such as the lungs, liver or the gastrointestinal tract. Malignant lymphocytes multiply uncontrollably and do not perform their normal functions. Hence, the body's ability to fight infections is affected. In addition, these malignant cells may crowd the bone marrow, and, depending on the stage, prevent the production of normal red blood

An anterior angled view of the lymphatic system. (© 3D4Medical/ Photo Researchers, Inc.)

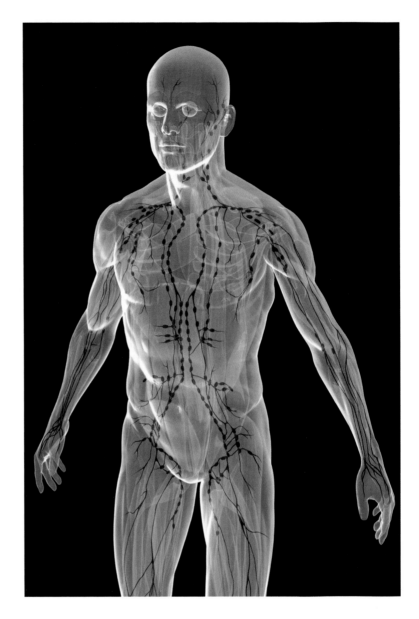

cells, white blood cells, and platelets. A low red blood cell count causes anemia, while a reduction in the number of platelets makes the person susceptible to excessive bleeding. Cancerous cells can also invade other organs through the circulatory system of the lymph, causing those organs to malfunction.

Causes and Symptoms

The exact cause of non-Hodgkin's lymphomas is not known. However, the incidence has increased significantly in recent years. Part of the increase is due to the AIDS epidemic. Individuals infected with the AIDS virus have a higher likelihood of developing non-Hodgkin's lymphomas. In general, males are at a higher risk for having non-Hodgkin's lymphomas than are females. The risk increases with age. Though it can strike people as young as 40, people between the ages of 60 and 69 are at the highest risk.

People exposed to certain pesticides and ionizing radiation have a higher than average chance of developing this disease. For example, an increased incidence of lymphomas has been seen in survivors of the atomic bomb explosion in Hiroshima [in 1945], and in people who have undergone aggressive radiation therapy. People who suffer from immune-deficient disorders, as well as those who have been treated with immune suppressive drugs for heart or kidney transplants, and for conditions such as rheumatoid arthritis and autoimmune diseases, are at an increased risk for this disease. . . .

The symptoms of lymphomas are often vague and non-specific. Patients may experience loss of appetite, weight loss, nausea, vomiting, abdominal discomfort, and indigestion. The patient may complain of a feeling of fullness, which is a result of enlarged lymph nodes in the abdomen. Pressure or pain in the lower back is another symptom. In the advanced stages, the patient may have bone pain, headaches, constant coughing, and abnormal pressure and congestion in the face, neck, and upper chest. Some may have fevers and night sweats. In most cases, patients go to the doctor because of the presence of swollen glands in the neck, armpits, or

> ## FAST FACT
>
> Lymphoma is the most common blood cancer. Of the three blood cancers (lymphoma, leukemia, and myeloma), 5 percent of new cases in 2010 were lymphoma, according to statistics supplied by the Leukemia & Lymphoma Society.

groin area. Since all the symptoms are common to many other illnesses, it is essential to seek medical attention if any of the conditions persist for two weeks or more. Only a qualified physician can correctly diagnose if the symptoms are due to lymphoma or some other ailment.

Diagnosis of Non-Hodgkin's Lymphoma

Like all cancers, lymphomas are best treated when found early. However, it is often difficult to diagnose lymphomas. There are no screening tests available, and, since the symptoms are non-specific, lymphomas are rarely recognized in their early stages. Detection often occurs by chance during a routine physical examination.

When the doctor suspects lymphoma, a complete medical history is taken, and a thorough physical examination is performed. Enlargement of the lymph nodes, liver, or spleen may suggest lymphomas. Blood tests will determine the cell counts and obtain information on how well the organs, such as the kidney and liver, are functioning.

A biopsy of the enlarged lymph node is the most definitive diagnostic tool for staging purposes. The doctor may perform a bone marrow biopsy. During the biopsy, a cylindrical piece of bone and marrow fluid is removed. They are generally taken out of the hipbone. These samples are sent to the laboratory for examination. In addition to diagnosis, the biopsy may also be repeated during the treatment phase of the disease to see if the lymphoma is responding to therapy.

Once the exact form of lymphoma is known, it is then staged to determine how aggressive it is, and how far it has spread. Staging is necessary to plan appropriate treatment.

Conventional imaging tests, such as x rays, computed tomography scans (CT scans), magnetic resonance imaging, and abdominal sonograms, are used to determine the extent of spread of the disease.

Major Non-Hodgkin's Lymphoma Types

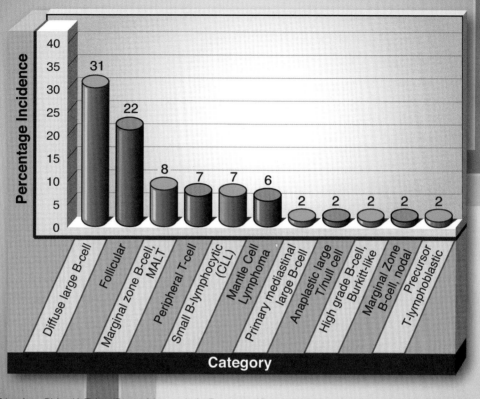

Taken from: Richard I. Fisher. "Recent Advances in the Treatment of Patients with Aggressive Non-Hodgkin's Lymphoma." Medscape Education, March 27, 2002. http://www.medscape.org.

Lymphangiograms are x rays of the lymphatic system. In this procedure, a special dye is injected into the lymphatic channels through a small cut (incision) made in each foot. The dye is injected slowly over a period of three to four hours. This dye clearly outlines the lymphatic system and allows it to stand out. Multiple x rays are then taken and any abnormality, if present, is revealed.

Rarely, a lumbar puncture or a spinal tap is performed to check if malignant cells are present in the fluid surrounding the brain. In this test, the physician inserts a needle into the epidural space at the base of the spine and collects a small amount of spinal fluid for microscopic examination.

Treatment options for lymphomas depend on the type of lymphoma and its present stage. In most cases, treatment consists of chemotherapy, radiotherapy, or a combination of the two methods. . . .

Prognosis and Prevention of Non-Hodgkin's Lymphomas

Like all cancers, the prognosis for lymphoma depends on the stage of the cancer, and the patient's age and general health. When all the different types and stages of lymphoma are considered together, only 50% of patients survive 5 years or more after initial diagnosis. This is because some types of lymphoma are more aggressive than others.

The survival rate among children is definitely better than among older people. About 90% of the children diagnosed with early stage disease survive 5 years or more, while only 60–70% of adults diagnosed with low grade lymphomas survive for 5 years or more. The survival rate for children with the more advanced stages is about 75–85%, while among adults it is 40–60%.

Although many cancers may be prevented by making diet and life style changes which reduce risk factors, there is currently no known way to prevent lymphomas. Protecting oneself from developing AIDS, which may be a risk factor for lymphomas, is the only preventive measure that can be practiced.

At present, there are no special tests that are available for early detection of non-Hodgkin's lymphomas. Paying prompt attention to the signs and symptoms of this disease, and seeing a doctor if the symptoms persist, are the best strategies for an early diagnosis of lymphoma. Early detection affords the best chance for a cure.

Risk Factors for Lymphoma

LymphomaInfo.net

LymphomaInfo.net is an Internet-based information resource for the lymphoma community that aims to bring people together around lymphoma-related issues by providing concise, up-to-date information and a meeting place for lymphoma patients and those who care about them.

In the following viewpoint the authors summarize the known risk factors for lymphoma. According to the authors, relevant factors include environmental risk factors (such as benzene, herbicides, and pesticides), immune system disorders such as HIV/AIDS, and certain infectious agents.

The causes of lymphoma are not well known. DNA mutations cause lymphoma to develop but what triggers these mutations is largely unknown. Family history does not provide much of a clue; except in the case of some rare forms, lymphoma does not appear to be linked to genetic inheritance.

SOURCE: "What Causes Lymphoma?," LymphomaInfo.net, n.d. Copyright © by LymphomaInfo.net. All rights reserved. Reproduced by permission.

However, as lymphoma incidence rises and research accelerates, several risk factors for lymphoma have been established. We outline some of them below. Please keep in mind that there are volumes of published research on the twenty to thirty known forms of lymphoma, and much remains to be learned. . . .

Environmental Risk Factors

It will probably not surprise you to learn that exposure to certain chemicals and radiation has been linked to lymphoma.

Solvents (Benzene). Chemical solvents such as acetone, alcohol (various alcohols, not just ethyl alcohol), toluene, xylene, turpentine, and benzene, are highly toxic and linked to lymphoma. Benzene exposure in particular, already a known cause of leukemia, is now linked to lymphoma and is the subject of much research and many lawsuits.

A meta-analysis of 22 benzene exposure studies by the UC [University of California] Berkeley School of Public Health concluded that, "The finding of elevated relative risks in studies of both benzene exposure and refinery work provides further evidence that benzene exposure causes NHL [Non-Hodgkin's lymphoma]." Benzene, a solvent manufactured from petroleum, is found in gasoline, cigarette smoke, and in many solvents. . . . Benzene exposure is also an occupational risk for oil industry jobs, particularly refining jobs, and plastics manufacturing.

Herbicides and Pesticides. Chemicals used for defoliation and pest control have been linked to lymphoma and are a significant risk factor. These chemicals are an occupational hazard for farmers and agricultural workers in particular. Populations in agricultural areas are also at significant risk from airborne exposure via crop dusting, and from groundwater exposure via contaminated water supplies. Herbicides and pesticides are also a potential threat to the general population who may ingest them through the food supply.

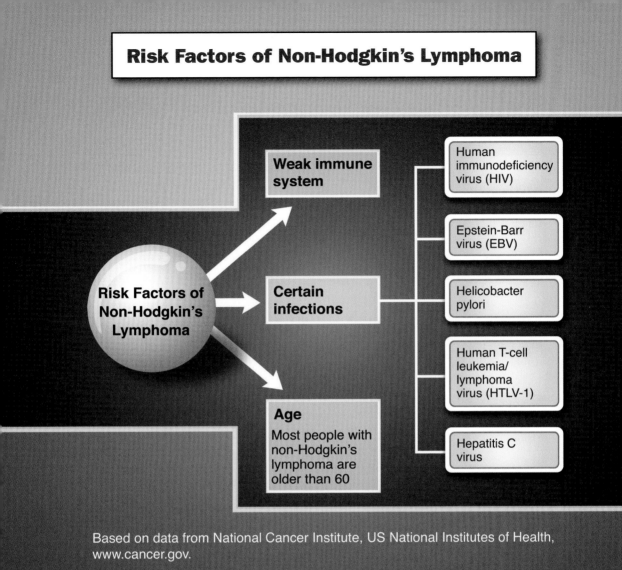

Risk Factors of Non-Hodgkin's Lymphoma

Risk Factors of Non-Hodgkin's Lymphoma

Weak immune system

Certain infections

Age
Most people with non-Hodgkin's lymphoma are older than 60

Human immunodeficiency virus (HIV)

Epstein-Barr virus (EBV)

Helicobacter pylori

Human T-cell leukemia/lymphoma virus (HTLV-1)

Hepatitis C virus

Based on data from National Cancer Institute, US National Institutes of Health, www.cancer.gov.

Taken from: "Risk Factors of Non-Hodgkin's Lymphoma." SmartDraw. http://www.smartdraw.com.

Agent Orange. "Agent Orange [AO]," named after the orange-striped drums used for shipping, refers to any of the phenoxy herbicides used for defoliation during the Vietnam War. Herbicides can enter the body not only from direct contact, but also through food and soil contamination and inhalation. Both soldiers and the Vietnamese population endured significant herbicide exposure. One herbicide in particular, 2,4,5-trichlorophenoxyacetic acid

[2,4,5-T], was particularly toxic because it contained dioxins. Dioxins remain in the environment—particularly the soil—for years and are linked to many cancers.

While it has not been irrefutably proven that exposure to Agent Orange causes cancer, the evidence is strong enough to put both Hodgkin's and non-Hodgkin's lymphoma on the U.S. Department of Veterans Affairs list of "Current Conditions Considered by VA [Veterans Affairs] Presumptive to AO Exposure."

Hair Dye. There has been a lot of press over the years linking hair dye to lymphoma and other cancers. Although there has been some inaccurate reporting on this issue, it is true that some link has been established, particularly in the case of hair dyes manufactured before 1980. A 2008 study of over 10,000 people published in the *American Journal of Epidemiology* (4,461 NHL patients and 5,799 controls) concluded the following:

> In summary, the results from this large InterLymph-based pooled analysis indicate that personal use of hair dye may play a role in the risk of NHL, particularly for follicular lymphoma and CLL/SLL [chronic lymphocytic leukemia/small lymphocytic lymphoma, two variations of the same disease]. Our study also indicates that although the risk associated with personal hair-dye use was observed mainly among women who started using hair dyes before 1980, the risk was not limited to those women. Future studies are needed to examine the risk of NHL by time period of hair-dye use and by genetic susceptibility.

Genetic Risk Factors

The genetic links to lymphoma are complicated and uncertain. Direct inheritance does not seem to be a factor. Even in the rare cases in which lymphoma occurs in fam-

FAST FACT

According to a 2009 article by Cancer Research UK, Hodgkin's lymphoma is eleven times more likely in people who are infected with the HIV virus or have AIDS.

ily clusters it is not clear whether genetics or environmental exposure—or a combination of the two—is the determining factor.

Inherited Immune Deficiencies. Lymphoma and genetics are most closely associated with inherited immune disorders. Lupus, rheumatoid arthritis, celiac disease and Sjögren's syndrome all appear to increase a person's chances of developing lymphoma.

Immune System Disorders

Lymphoma is essentially an immune system disease and positive correlations exist between many immune deficiencies and various lymphomas.

HIV/AIDS. The incidence of lymphoma in HIV/AIDS patients is substantially higher than that of the general population, so much so that the condition, usually a type

Exposure to certain chemicals, such as solvents, herbicides, and pesticides, has been linked to lymphoma.
(© Wayne G. Lawler/ Photo Researchers, Inc.)

of B-Cell lymphoma, has its own description: "AIDS-related lymphoma." It is still the same cancer suffered by HIV-negative patients, but demands special attention because it is so closely linked to the virus. HIV patients are determined to have AIDS when they develop significant conditions and/or diseases in conjunction with the virus; lymphoma is frequently a determining factor.

Epstein-Barr Virus. Epstein-Barr virus [EBV], a member of the herpes virus family, is extremely common and can result in infectious mononucleosis in young adults. In most cases EBV infection and "mono" are not serious conditions. However, in patients with compromised immune systems in which T-cells do not destroy infected B-cells, EBV-infected cells may become cancerous. The strongest correlation between lymphoma and EBV pertains to Burkitt's lymphoma.

Helicobacter Pylori. H. Pylori is bacteria found in populations worldwide. It can result in minor stomach inflammation, ulcers, and can lead to stomach cancer. *H. Pylori* is also linked to MALT [mucosa associated lymphoid tissue] lymphoma, a rare type of B-cell tumor.

Current Treatments for Lymphoma

Mark R. Fesen

Mark R. Fesen is an oncologist and internist with fifteen years of clinical practice caring for patients with lymphoma and other cancers. He is a graduate of Robert Wood Johnson Medical School and a fellow of the American College of Physicians. He has trained at the National Cancer Institute and is a clinical assistant professor at the University of Kansas.

In the following viewpoint Fesen describes a number of therapeutic interventions for lymphoma, including standard treatments such as radiation and chemotherapy, as well as newer treatments such as monoclonal antibodies. He also discusses complications that can arise either from lymphoma itself or from the treatments, and how such complications are dealt with.

Lymphomas are divided into many different types, including Hodgkin's and non-Hodgkin's classes. Hodgkin's disease . . . is highly curable in many

SOURCE: Mark R. Fesen, *Surviving the Cancer System: An Empowering Guide to Taking Control of Your Care.* New York: American Management Association, 2009, pp. 197–201. Copyright © 2009 by American Management Association. All rights reserved. Reproduced by permission.

patients, even when it is advanced. Hodgkin's disease was the first example of a cancer where combinations of chemotherapy were developed that were able to cure patients.

In the past, many younger women in their teens and twenties were treated with radiation therapy. One goal of this was to avoid chemotherapy and keep the women fertile. Often this radiation included treatments to the chest and breasts. These resulted in the women being cured of their Hodgkin's. Unfortunately, the radiation therapy increased the women's chances of developing breast cancer.

There are more than ten different subclasses of non-Hodgkin's lymphomas, but for the purposes of treatment there are usually three major types. The first is slow growing and is known as the indolent lymphomas. These initially grow at a very slow rate but often recur. Over time, their unstable DNA can mutate and transform into more aggressive types of lymphomas.

Indolent lymphomas are initially very responsive to even minimal chemotherapy and radiation treatments. Even without any intervention, it is not unusual for a patient to survive up to ten years. It is also common to not even need any treatment with these slow growing lymphomas, although oncologists are becoming more aggressive about treating them. A cure for indolent lymphomas has remained difficult to achieve. Even after remission, these lymphomas eventually return in most patients. Newer treatment strategies employ a combination of intravenous chemotherapy drugs along with monoclonal antibodies. Treanda (bendamustine) is a drug recently approved for the treatment of non-Hodgkin's lymphoma.

Monoclonal Antibodies

Monoclonal antibodies are examples of targeted therapies directed toward the specific chemicals, called receptors, on the surface of lymphoma cells. These antibodies

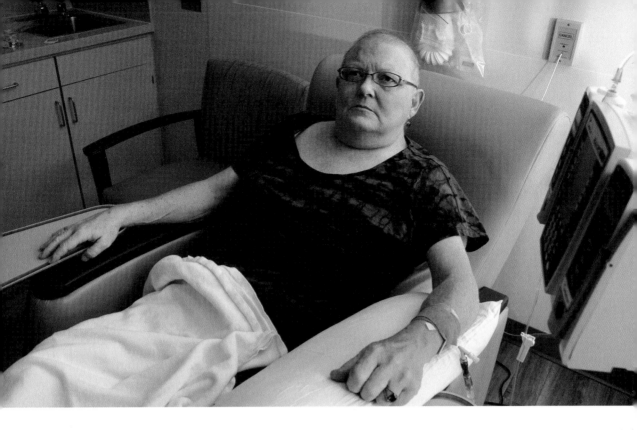

can be either cold and not radioactive or hot and linked to a particle of radiation, but in the majority of cases, cold antibodies are used. No special radiation precautions are needed. These cold antibodies are given in the medical oncology office. One example is a drug named Rituxan (rituximab). These targeted antibodies are key to improving the chances of many lymphoma patients to both get into and stay in remission.

Cold, or nonradioactive, antibodies have several advantages over the hot antibodies. They can easily be given repeatedly without concern about accumulating a total dose of radiation. Repeated doses of these drugs will severely lower the white blood cell counts. This rarely occurs with the cold targeted drug, rituximab. The nonradioactive antibodies also are much less likely to contribute to a radiation-caused leukemia or cancer. Although this is a theoretical risk and may take years to develop, it can occur. Leukemias and other cancers caused by radiation or chemotherapy are expected to be very difficult to treat.

Many lymphomas are treated with chemotherapy, although the treatment poses risks for some patients.
(© age fotostock/ SuperStock)

Lymphomas can be indolent diseases, which means they may last from a few years to ten or fifteen years. Over time, the lymphoma cells naturally become more resistant to treatments. This resistance often develops when standard chemotherapy drugs are used. Use of antibodies, such as the drug Rituxan (rituximab), however, allows a long holiday from chemotherapy. This helps the body's bone marrow function to recover and minimizes the exposure to chemotherapy drugs. During the protracted time in which the lymphoma is kept in remission by such antibody drugs, patients generally suffer few, if any, symptoms from either their disease or their treatment. As is the case with many cancer patients, quality of life is better when the disease is inactive. Also, by staying in remission, you avoid the complications and symptoms of the disease of lymphoma itself, as well as the need for re-treatment with combination chemotherapy.

FAST FACT

A 2010 article in London's *Telegraph* notes that the chance of surviving large-cell lymphoma has increased from less than 50 percent to over 75 percent in the past decade.

Concerns About Radiation

When the monoclonal antibodies are linked to radiation particles, several concerns arise. The radiation can affect your body's bone marrow function, thereby limiting your resistance to infections. The radiation exposure may also, over time, induce a higher chance of developing a second leukemia. Zevalin (ibritumomab tiuxetan) and Bexxar (tositumomab and iodine I-131 tositumomab) are examples of two of these drugs.

Lymphoma can cause many symptoms. These include fevers, chills, night sweats, and fatigue. Other symptoms common to the slow growing lymphomas are kidney failure as a result of blockage of the tubes called ureters that drain the urine from the kidney. Less common are blood clots and strokes caused by changes to the blood's likelihood to clot. At times, pain or numbness can be caused by lymphoma pinching off nerves that travel to arms and legs. Lymphomas can also occur in the bowel and cause vague symptoms. These include diarrhea, constipation, or trouble with nutrition. Lymphomas confined to the intestine can be very challenging to diagnose. At times surgeons will try to both diagnose and remove these bowel lymphomas. Limiting the surgery and relying on chemotherapy and monoclonal antibodies for treatment seems to be the better approach. Newer molecular biological tests that test the receptors on the surface of the cancer cells, known as flow cytometry, can diagnose lymphoma in the intestine using only a small sample obtained during an endoscopy. (An endoscopy

Risks for Hodgkin's Lymphoma Patients Receiving Both Radiation and Chemotherapy

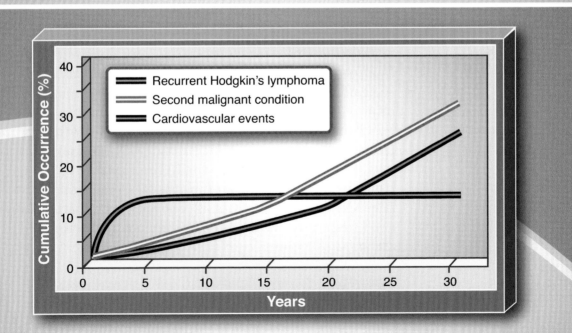

Taken from: James O. Acmitage, "Early-Stage Hodgkin's Lymphoma," *New England Journal of Medicine*, 2010. http://www.nejm.org/doi/full/10, 1056/NEJMra1003733.

is when a small telescope is used to examine the patient's stomach or intestines.)

T-Cell and Intermediate Grade Lymphomas

Lymphomas can also begin outside the lymph nodes in unusual places. These areas include the brain, skin, lung, cervix, and throat. When they begin in the skin, they can appear as long-term nonhealing patches or tumors that are known as T-cell lymphomas. These may grow over several years and are treated with an entirely different group of both chemotherapy and molecularly targeted drugs. Targretin (Bexarotene), Ontak (denileukin diftitox), and Zolinza (vorinostat) are examples of drugs for T-cell lymphomas.

Intermediate grade lymphomas are also common. Fortunately these lymphomas are more curable than the slow growing variety. Because this type of lymphoma is more curable, the treatments are more intense and regimented. Depending on the stage of the lymphoma, either chemotherapy or chemotherapy and radiation will be used. The combinations of drugs employed vary, but usually four or five drugs are given every three weeks for four to six months. Again, monoclonal antibodies directed against receptors on the surface of the lymphoma cells improve survival chances.

Chemotherapy can be especially effective with lymphomas. In this circumstance a complication known as tumor lysis syndrome may occur. This is where so many lymphoma cells are killed off by the treatments that they affect the body's other organs. The kidneys in particular need to be protected from this effect by hydration and certain medications.

Treating Complications of Lymphoma

Patients who are suffering from lymphomas develop particular types of complications from the disease and the treatment. In addition to certain infections, other complications often include certain pneumonias because of the compromised immune system from the lymphoma. Antibiotics may be given once or twice a week during treatments to prevent these pneumonias. Other infections that occur commonly are viral, such as cold sores in the mouth or shingles. The chance of contracting shingles can be diminished if the patient has been vaccinated or if he or she is able to take a further medication to prevent it. Shingles shows up as a close group of blisters on a red base on only one side of the body, usually in a band. After the rash and infection, it leaves many patients with the dreaded postherpetic neuralgia or the shingles pain syndrome. Avoid the pain syndrome by recognizing the rash and starting on the shingles antiviral pain medicine as soon as possible. Yeast infections in the mouth, skin, and genitals also are commonly seen in lymphoma patients. Early treatment helps here also.

Other important complications when treating lymphoma patients include toxicities from certain drugs. One commonly used is vincristine. This drug can cause a paralyzed bowel known as an ileus. The bloating that develops is very uncomfortable but can be prevented with laxatives. Numbness in the hands can also occur with vincristine, as with many other drugs.

The time it takes to cure intermediate grade non-Hodgkin's lymphoma patients is usually several months. Additionally, a certain number of patients don't respond completely to the standard combination of the four chemotherapy agents, cyclophosphamide, vincristine, doxorubicin and prednisone, or the lymphoma returns at a later time. When Rituxan (rituximab) is routinely added to this combination, the chance of cure improves. Protocols using combinations of other second-line drugs are also available. These can be combined with stem cell bone marrow transplants to further improve chances of survival.

Antibody Combination Therapy Shows Great Promise in Treating Lymphoma

Krista Conger

Krista Conger is a science writer at Stanford University. In the following viewpoint Conger describes a promising research program using a combination of antibodies (rituximab and anti-CD47) to treat lymphoma by helping the body's immune system to attack and kill cancer cells. Rituximab is an antibody treatment currently in use that binds to lymphoma cells, enabling the immune system to identify and eat the cells. However, blood cancer cells often produce a substance called CD47 that sends a "don't-eat-me" signal to the immune system. The anti-CD47 antibody blocks that signal, allowing the immune system to attack and kill the lymphoma cells. According to Conger, the study showed that using rituximab and anti-CD47 at the same time created a synergistic healing effect that was far more powerful than using either antibody treatment alone. So far the treatment has been tested in mice, but the researchers are hopeful that it will work in humans as well.

SOURCE: Krista Conger, "New Antibody-Combination Therapy Developed at Stanford Boosts Human Lymphoma Cure Rate in Mouse Models," *States News Service,* September 2, 2010. http://med .stanford.edu/ism/2010/september/cd47.html. Copyright © 2010 by the Stanford University School of Medicine Office of Communication & Public Affairs. Reproduced with permission.

More than half of laboratory mice with human non-Hodgkin's lymphoma [NHL] are cured by a treatment involving just two monoclonal antibodies, researchers at the Stanford University School of Medicine have found. The therapy combines the activity of rituximab, an antibody currently in use to treat the disorder, with another that blocks a molecule called CD47 on the surface of the cancer cells. Together the two antibodies synergize to trigger the host's own immune system to eliminate the cancer.

"What we're seeing is that we have a potential therapy for non-Hodgkin's lymphoma that can eliminate the disease in mice even without chemotherapy," said the co-first author of the research, MD/PhD student Mark Chao. Currently, about 30 percent of patients with NHL die of the disease.

Because many cancer cells express elevated levels of CD47, the researchers hope that the potential therapeutic benefit shown in this study by the combination therapy will also extend to other types of cancers.

The findings of this study lay the groundwork for trials in humans. Last October [2009], the researchers received a $20 million Disease Team Grant from the California Institute for Regenerative Medicine [CIRM] to bring the new antibody therapy into clinical trials in human patients with a related cancer—acute myeloid leukemia—within four to five years.

"The goal is to get the immune system to target and kill cancer cells," said Ravindra Majeti, MD, PhD, an assistant professor of hematology at the medical school and a study co-author. "We found that, although treating the mice with either antibody alone was somewhat beneficial, treating with both antibodies simultaneously cured the mice in over 60 percent of the cases."

The research is published in the Sept. 3 [2010] issue of *Cell*. Majeti and Irving Weissman, MD, director of Stanford's Institute for Stem Cell Biology and Regenerative

Medicine, are co-senior authors of the study. Chao and acting assistant professor of oncology Ash Alizadeh, MD, PhD, are co-first authors of the work. Weissman and Majeti are co-principal investigators on the CIRM grant and are both members of the Stanford Cancer Center.

A Synergistic Combination

"We want to bring this to patients as quickly as we can," said Chao. The researchers point out that, although the CIRM grant focuses on investigating anti-CD47 therapies for acute myeloid leukemia, the drug development process will result in an antibody that could also be used for other cancers. They focused their preliminary investigations on non-Hodgkin's lymphoma because they were curious as to how the anti-CD47 antibody would work with rituximab, which also binds to human lymphoma cells.

FAST FACT

A study published in the November 4, 2010, issue of the *New England Journal of Medicine* reported that complete or partial remissions were produced in 38 percent of patients with therapy-resistant or relapsed Hodgkin's lymphoma when they were treated with an antibody combined with an anti-cancer agent.

"Biologically, it makes sense that these two antibodies would work together," said Majeti. "One, rituximab, binds to the lymphoma cells and serves as an activator for cells of the immune system. The other, anti-CD47, blocks a 'don't-eat-me' signal these blood cancer cells use to evade the immune cells as they move throughout the body. But we were amazed at the robustness of the synergy between the two."

Rituximab alone does not cure human patients with NHL. It must be combined with chemotherapy—and even then it does not always work. "A major limitation of our current therapeutic approaches is a lack of increasingly active agents for the most aggressive lymphomas," said Alizadeh, who treats lymphoma patients at Stanford Hospital and Clinics. "Rituximab is the biggest advance that's been made in the last 30 years. But even so, we lose about one-third of patients with systemic disease."

Blocking a Cancer Cell's "Don't-Eat-Me" Signal

CD47 came to the attention of the researchers in 2008 when Chao, Majeti and Weissman found that the molecule protected human leukemia cells from engulfment and destruction by a protective immune cell called a macrophage. Because many cancer cells have higher-than-normal levels of CD47 on their surface, the researchers speculated that an antibody that binds to CD47

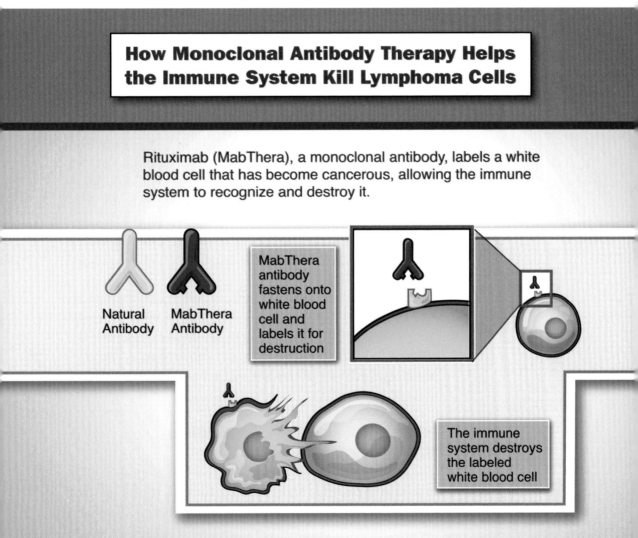

How Monoclonal Antibody Therapy Helps the Immune System Kill Lymphoma Cells

Rituximab (MabThera), a monoclonal antibody, labels a white blood cell that has become cancerous, allowing the immune system to recognize and destroy it.

Natural Antibody

MabThera Antibody

MabThera antibody fastens onto white blood cell and labels it for destruction

The immune system destroys the labeled white blood cell

Taken from: "Treatment for Indolent NHL." *EPG Patient Direct*, September 14, 2007. http://www.epgpatientdirect.org.

and masks its appearance might allow the macrophages to go back to happily munching on the rogue cells.

Indeed, Alizadeh found that people whose lymphoma cells expressed higher levels of CD47 had a worse prognosis than did those whose cancer cells expressed lower levels of CD47. In particular, those with a form of the disease called diffuse large B cell lymphoma were significantly more likely to die of their disease if their cells had more of the molecule on their surface. Interestingly, he found that high CD47 expression correlates with other, previously identified prognostic factors.

"We've known, for example, that the cell-of-origin for these lymphomas is an important indicator of how a patient is likely to respond to therapy," said Alizadeh. "But until now we've had no way to try to address that therapeutically."

The scientists tested their theory in human non-Hodgkin's lymphoma primary cells and cell lines in culture dishes and in laboratory mice. They first showed that incubating human NHL cells in a culture dish with either mouse or human macrophages in the presence of anti-CD47 significantly increased the ability of the macrophages to eat and kill the cancer cells, and that this killing ability varied according to the levels of CD47 expressed on the cells' surfaces.

Incubating the cells with rituximab had a similar effect. However, using both antibodies together dramatically increased the macrophages' ability to wipe out the lymphoma cells in a way that was more than additive—that is, the activity of the anti-CD47 antibody and rituximab was synergistic.

Combining the Two Therapies Was Much More Effective

When the researchers injected mice intravenously with cells from the human NHL cell line, the cells multiplied and the animals developed disseminated lymphoma. The eight

mice treated with a control antibody all had to be euthanized due to tumor burden in just over 20 days. Although treating the mice with either rituximab or anti-CD47 decreased the number of tumor cells and prolonged the animals' survival (to about 30 days), they eventually all died of the disease. But when the animals were treated with the combination antibody therapy, five out of eight mice lived for more than 180 days with no evidence of tumor cells.

Similar results were seen when the cells were injected into the flanks of mice, where they formed palpable tumors. Short-term treatment with the combination of the two antibodies allowed six out of seven of the animals to achieve a complete remission that lasted for more than 190 days, when the experiment was stopped.

Finally, because cell lines can accumulate genetic changes over time that differ from primary cells, the researchers repeated the experiments using cells isolated

A technician removes antibody-producing cell clones from a cryo container, in which they were preserved at an extremely low temperature. Used in monoclonal antibody therapy, the cells help the immune system kill lymphoma cells. (© AP Images/Winifred Rothermel)

directly from human patients with NHL. They found that eight out of nine mice injected with diffuse large B cell lymphoma and then subsequently treated with the two antibodies lived for more than four months without evidence of disease. In contrast, all animals treated with the control antibody, or with either antibody alone, had to be euthanized due to progression of their disease.

The researchers are . . . moving ahead as quickly as possible to bring the anti-CD47 antibody treatment to trials in human patients.

"We first found this molecule when we compared leukemia stem cells in mice with their normal counterparts," said Weissman, who is also a professor of pathology. "It is amazing to me that this new approach to cancer stem cells in mice showed us the most important hidden component of how the body is likely to attack all cancers—the macrophage—and how human cancers evade killing by using the 'don't-eat-me' signal. Blocking this signal and adding an 'eat-me' signal to the lymphoma cells is the next step in therapy.

"Let's hope that this treatment that cures lymphoma in mice will cure it in humans, but we must remember that we are still many steps from a clinical trial in humans," Weissman added. "Many other exciting potential therapies have failed in humans."

"In many ways this is a labor of love," said Alizadeh. "It is a very humbling experience to walk into an exam room and tell a patient with lymphoma that you've run out of bullets to shoot at their cancer and to prepare them to give up. Hopefully, this work will be a testament to how hard we're all trying to help such patients."

CHAPTER 2

Controversies Surrounding Lymphoma

Chemotherapy Is an Effective and Often Lifesaving Treatment for Hodgkin's Lymphoma

David Gorski

David Gorski is a surgical oncologist at the Barbara Ann Karmanos Cancer Institute, where he also serves as the American College of Surgeons Committee on Cancer liaison physician as well as an associate professor of surgery and member of the faculty of the Graduate Program in Cancer Biology at Wayne State University.

In the following viewpoint Gorski argues that although chemotherapy has many unpleasant and unhealthy side effects, it is also highly effective at treating blood-based cancers such as Hodgkin's lymphoma. He points out the terrible effects of untreated cancer and suggests that people who reject chemotherapy as a treatment for their lymphoma will increase their risk of dying from the disease, as well as increase suffering due to disease symptoms. According to Gorski, even when cancer is terminal it is better to have chemotherapy to reduce the painful symptoms of the disease.

Photo on previous page. Though chemotherapy causes acute nausea, as well as baldness, it is considered by many experts to be the best available treatment for cancer. (© Phanie/Photo Researchers, Inc.)

SOURCE: David Gorski, "Chemotherapy Versus Death from Cancer," *Science-Based Medicine*, April 19, 2010. www.Science BasedMedicine.org. Copyright © 2010 by Science-Based Medicine. All rights reserved. Reproduced by permission.

I've written before about the Daniel Hauser case, a 13 year old boy who last year [2009] refused chemotherapy for his Hodgkin's lymphoma, necessitating the involvement of the legal system. Cases like that of Daniel Hauser represent supreme "teachable" moments that—fortunately—don't come along that often . . . cases like that of Daniel Hauser tend to pop up only once every couple of years or even less. As tragic as they are, they always bring up so many issues that I have a hard time leaving them alone.

This time around, I wanted to touch on an issue that has come up frequently in the discussions of this case, and that's the issue of chemotherapy. Specifically, it's the issue of how horrible chemotherapy can be. Again, make no mistake about it, chemotherapy can be rough. Very rough. But what is often forgotten is that it can also be life-saving, particularly in the case of hematologic malignancies [blood-based cancers such as lymphoma], where it is the primary therapy. What is also often forgotten or intentionally ignored by promoters of unscientific medicine is that doctors don't use chemotherapy because they have some perverted love of "torturing" patients, because they're in the pockets of big pharma and looking for cash, or because they are too lazy to find another way. They do it because, at least right now, it's the best therapy science-based medicine has to offer, and in the case of Hodgkin's lymphoma, for example, it's life-saving. You can be sure that if a less harsh way were found to achieve the same results, physicians would jump all over it. Indeed, a major focus of oncology research these days is to find less brutal regimens and improve the quality of life of cancer patients while still giving them the best shot at survival.

Chemotherapy Has Terrible Side Effects

Yes, chemotherapy can make you feel nauseated and make you throw up. It can make your hair fall out. It can temporarily depress the immune system. It can cause

Chemotherapy's Optimal Therapeutic Range

If chemotherapy dosage is too low, it may not effectively eliminate the cancer cells; if too high, the powerful drugs will cause unacceptable damage to the patient. Caregivers aim for the optimal therapeutic range for the medication, based on the type and stage of lymphoma and the condition of the patient.

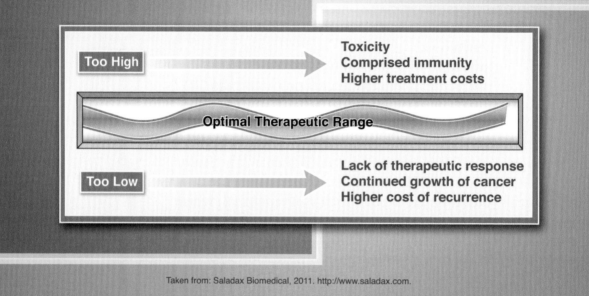

Too High → Toxicity / Comprised immunity / Higher treatment costs

Optimal Therapeutic Range

Too Low → Lack of therapeutic response / Continued growth of cancer / Higher cost of recurrence

Taken from: Saladax Biomedical, 2011. http://www.saladax.com.

bleeding complications, such as GI [gastrointestinal] bleeding. It can cause kidney damage. It can cause heart damage. It can cause lung damage. It can cause nerve damage. It can make you lose weight. It can even result in your death from complications. In short, it is not something to be used lightly. Unfortunately, the disease it's meant to fight is a formidable foe indeed. It is your own cells, and all too often the difference between the toxicity of chemotherapy against the cancer and against normal cells is not that large.

But what does cancer do? How do cancer patients die? They suffer and die in protean [highly variable and unpredictable] ways. Cancer can do everything chemotherapy can do (with the exception of hair loss) and more. I've seen more patients than I care to know suffer and die from cancer. I've seen family members suffer and die from cancer, most recently my mother-in-law last year.

One of the most frequent claims of cancer patients who opt for quackery instead of chemotherapy and effective science-based therapies is that they want to remain healthy. Some, as Abraham Cherrix [another teenage lymphoma patient who refused chemotherapy] did, state that, even if they end up dying, they want to "die healthy." It's a dangerous delusion. There is nothing "healthy" about dying from cancer. Dying from cancer is anything but "healthy." But it is perfectly natural, as natural (or even more so) than the herbal concoctions that so many alt-med believers put their faith into. But what does dying from untreated cancer mean? What happens? What does it involve?

Untreated Cancer Has Horrific Effects

Dying from untreated cancer can mean unrelenting pain that leaves you the choice of being drugged up with narcotics or being in agony.

Dying from untreated cancer can mean unrelenting vomiting from a bowel obstruction. It can mean having a nasogastric tube to drain your digestive juices and prevent you from throwing up. Alternatively, it can mean having to have a tube sticking out of your stomach to drain its fluids.

Dying from untreated cancer can mean bleeding because you don't have enough platelets to clot. The bleeding can come in many forms. It can be bleeding into the brain, in essence a hemorrhagic stroke. It can mean bleeding from the rectum or vomiting blood incessantly. And, because so many transfusions are all too often necessary, immune reactions can chew up new platelets as fast as they're infused. Yes, paradoxically, even when a cancer patient's immune system is suppressed in late stage cancer, frequently it does work against the one thing you don't want it to: Transfusions of blood products.

Dying from untreated cancer can mean horrific cachexia [ongoing weight loss]. Think Nazi concentration camp survivor, think starving Africans. Think famine. Think having cheeks so sunken that your face looks like the skull underlying it.

Dying from untreated cancer can mean your lungs progressively filling with fluid from tumor infiltration. Think choking on your own secretions. Think a progressive shortness of breath. Think an unrelenting feeling of suffocation but with no possibility of relief ever. . . .

Dying from cancer can mean a progressive decline in mental function due to brain metastases.

Dying from cancer can mean so many other horrific things happening to you that they are way too numerous to include a comprehensive list in a blog post. . . .

Modern Medicine Reduces Suffering

Modern medicine can alleviate many of the symptoms people with terminal cancer suffer, but all too often it can't reverse the disease process. However, the relief of these symptoms requires that the patient actually accept treatment. Hospice can minimize such symptoms, often for significant periods of time. However, even with the very best hospice care, there is nothing "healthy" or pleasant about dying from cancer. It means a loss of control. It can mean being too weak to get up by yourself, to feed yourself, to go to the bathroom yourself, to bathe yourself, or to do much other than lie in your bed and wait for the end. Without such treatment, a patient who chooses quackery over effective curative or palliative therapy dooms himself to a painful and unpleasant death. He in effect dooms himself to the sorts of ends untreated cancer patients suffered hundreds of years ago, before there was effective therapy. It doesn't have to be this way, but the seductive promise of a cure without pain, without hair falling out, without nausea lures cancer patients to havens of quackery in Tijuana [Mexico] or to flee from authorities trying to see that a child obtains potentially life-saving treatment, all because of a magnified fear of chemotherapy, all because of the propaganda that paints chemotherapy as "poison," radiation as "burning," and surgery as "slashing."

Here's the dirty little secret behind "alternative cancer cure" (ACC) promises. They are seductive because it is true that cancer patients who stop their chemotherapy will feel better than they did when undergoing chemotherapy. Of course they do, at least for a while! Often what happens, as in Daniel Hauser's case, is that the tumor shrinks, and, once the chemotherapy course is done, the patient does feel better because the tumor is no longer causing B symptoms [night sweats, fever and weight loss associated with lymphoma] or compressing lungs and making him short of breath, and other symptoms are also relieved. It is also true that more chemotherapy will make the patient feel lousy again for a time. Unfortunately, in the case of Hodgkin's lymphoma, the additional chemotherapy is necessary to maximize the chance of cure. Hodgkin's disease frequently relapses without the additional courses of chemotherapy. Science and clinical trials have told us that. Daniel Hauser is living proof, an anecdote that is consistent with what science tells us.

In other words, the promise of ACCs is a lie. They promise that cancer patients will always feel the way they do after the first course of chemotherapy is over and they have recovered or the way they feel before the tumor has grown beyond what can be cured. They are either deluded or lying. That's because cancer doesn't give up. It's like the Terminator [movie character cyborg]. It can't be bargained with. It can't be reasoned with. It doesn't feel pity, or remorse, or fear. And, if it is not treated, it absolutely will not stop, ever, until the patient is dead. And it rarely will be a pretty end. There's a case to be made that it isn't worth the symptoms to undergo chemotherapy when it has a very small chance of success. Such a judgment is up to the patient, based on his or her values and an accurate knowledge of the risks and benefits, which we as science-based physicians must provide them. However, all too often, by foregoing effective palliation, patients who choose ACCs condemn themselves to an end far more brutal than is necessary even if their cancer is terminal when diagnosed, and patients whose cancer is not terminal when diagnosed give up their one best shot at life.

Alternative Cancer Treatments Are a Dangerous Distraction from Effective Conventional Treatment for Hodgkin's Lymphoma and Other Cancers

Society for Integrative Oncology

The Society for Integrative Oncology (SIO) is a nonprofit, multidisciplinary organization for health professionals committed to the study and application of complementary therapies and botanicals for cancer patients.

In the following viewpoint the authors discuss a case in which a young teenager with Hodgkin's lymphoma and his parents rejected chemotherapy in favor of an unproven alternative treatment. The SIO authors support proven therapies that complement conventional treatment but argue that rejecting conventional treatment altogether means giving up the best hope for a cure. According to the authors, health care practitioners need to understand why people sometimes abandon conventional treatment and to engage patients in compassionate, respectful dialogue about their beliefs in order to encourage them to keep proven conventional therapies at the center of their treatment plan.

SOURCE: "Abandonment of the Conventional Oncology System: The Daniel Hauser Case," Society for Integrative Oncology, 2009. www.integrativeonc.org. Copyright © 2009 by Society for Integrative Oncology. All rights reserved. Reproduced by permission.

Hodgkin's lymphoma is a highly curable form of cancer when treated with chemotherapy and radiation. But Daniel Hauser (a young teenager) and his parents rejected chemotherapy after a single treatment, with the boy's mother saying that putting toxic substances in the body violates the family's religious convictions. Daniel's mother said she had been treating the boy's cancer instead with herbal supplements, vitamins, ionized water and other natural alternatives—a regimen based mostly on information she found on the Internet. Since then the disease has advanced, and Daniel's mother has abducted him away from his concerned oncologist in Minnesota.

The Society for Integrative Oncology advocates the best scientifically proven standards for cancer treatment and distinguishes clearly between helpful evidence-based and safe complementary therapies used to reduce symptoms and to help patients cope, in contrast to so-called alternative therapies that are bogus interventions often promoted for commercial gain. In this case, the Hausers have pursued a path of alternative therapies which cannot be condoned by any rational arguments.

So why do some patients turn to alternative therapies? There are multiple reasons including exasperation with the treatment they have received in traditional care modalities, are terrified of the adverse reactions to conventional therapies, or desperate for a cure, having been told that their cancer is incurable. In this case, it would appear that the oncology staff were exceedingly compassionate and concerned, and had indicated clearly the high probability of cure with chemotherapy, albeit with adverse effects that are minimized as much as possible.

Alternative Therapies Are Rarely Successful

Alternative therapies provide short-term hope, but are not usually successful. With few anecdotal exceptions, if conventional therapies offer an evidence-based opportu-

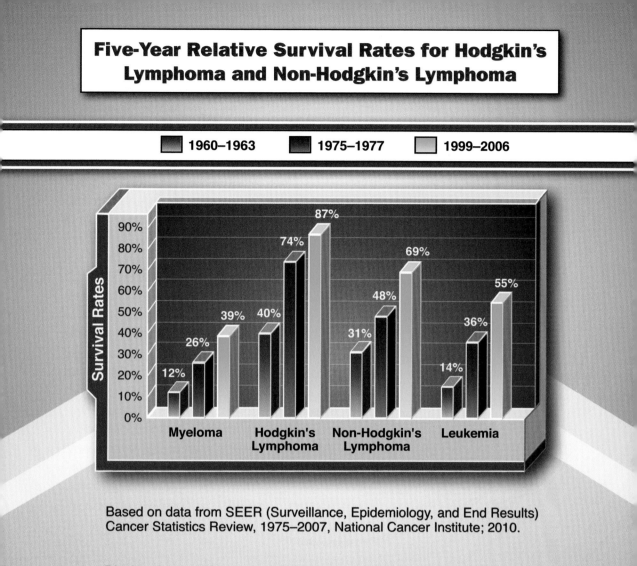

Five-Year Relative Survival Rates for Hodgkin's Lymphoma and Non-Hodgkin's Lymphoma

■ 1960–1963　　■ 1975–1977　　□ 1999–2006

Based on data from SEER (Surveillance, Epidemiology, and End Results) Cancer Statistics Review, 1975–2007, National Cancer Institute; 2010.

Taken from: "Facts and Statistics." Leukemia and Lymphoma Society, March 23, 2011. http://www.lls.org.

nity for long-term benefit, then substituting an unproven alternative treatment may result in losing the best opportunity for survival. This is clearly futile gambling with one's life and diminished personal responsibility. Pundits for alternative therapies often argue that they have been suppressed by the establishment, despite the fact that the Office of Cancer Complementary and Alternative Medicine of the National Cancer Institute (OCCAM) provides ample opportunity for innovative research on best case series. Unjustified Pollyanna branding of alternative therapies has negatively influenced patients in deciding to enter clinical trials.

The term "complementary therapy" (or "complementary medicine") is to be distinguished from "alternative medicine." Historically, the two are bundled together under the term "complementary and alternative therapies" (CAM). Alternative therapies are typically promoted as viable treatment options: "alternatives" to so-called mainstream therapies such as chemotherapy, radiation, and surgery. Alternative therapies are unproved, rarely based on credible scientific rationale, and potentially harmful—especially when patients are led away from effective, proven therapies by the lure of false promises and an emphasis on a lack of adverse side effects as compared with conventional therapies. There is no alternative to scientifically evaluated, evidence-based medicine. Most patients who use unconventional therapies (all but 2%) do so to complement rather than to replace mainstream treatment. However, because of desperation or fear, or because of inadequate support and communication, patients may seek alternative therapies.

Why People Abandon Conventional Treatment

Research studies conclude that patients who abandon conventional biomedical treatments do so for the following reasons:

1. *Anger and fear.* The patient may be angry at the health care system or their physician. Others may fear the clinical health care environment, adverse side effects, or the blunt presentation of prognosis. Some patients may not be able to cope because of underlying depression.

2. *Lack of control.* Some patients may feel a loss of control in the conventional health care system, whereas a primary alternative approach can give them a sense of empowerment. On the other hand, open-decision making may be overwhelming, and some patients give themselves over to the alternative practitioner.

3. *Belief in a cure.* The alternative approach may provide a more positive belief system for cure. A negative prognostic approach by a conventional practitioner may persuade a patient to seek an alternative therapy that is unjustly branded as delivering a cure.

4. *Social group association.* A peer group of social support may be very persuasive at encouraging alternative therapies, based on misinformation but the urge to be helpful.

5. *Mysticism.* Healing symbols and spiritual healing give some patients the feelings of control and coping. This may carry them through the rough places of their experiences, cushioning them against fears.

This is not just a North American problem. Worldwide, many patients may be deprived of effective modern anticancer therapies secondary to primitive cultural beliefs and a lack of modern resources. In developing countries, factors such as ignorance, socioeconomics, and inadequate access to mainstream medical facilities are some major factors that play an important role in patients opting for alternative therapies that are replacements for, rather than adjuncts to, mainstream therapy. Communication between patients and health professionals appears to be the major cause of biomedical abandonment. The research by [Muriel] Montebriand et al. contains numerous instances of angry confrontations and inadequate communication strategies by health professionals. When diagnosed with cancer, patients are vulnerable and emotions are easily stimulated. Anger may arise within the consultation. Health professionals may distance themselves from the anxiety of the cancer situation. Both verbal and nonverbal messages can be interpreted as lack of interest and lack of hope. Conversely, the informants believe they receive hope when communicating with alternative practitioners.

More Effective Communication Is Needed

Exclusive use of alternate therapies is often associated with hope for a cure and unresolved personal issues or unrealized biomedical expectations. Health professionals need improved communication skills; medical information should give hope. Spiritual isues should be addressed, utilizing representatives from the religious community as champions for good quality health care. Patients bring more than just their concerns about cancer to the clinical situation. They bring present and past experiences, social schemata, and spiritual interpretation. Patients should be encouraged to express their personal perceptions of health care. Frank and caring communication can happen only if professionals take time to listen (without anger), especially when patients discuss alternatives. Negative biomedical experiences, such as iatrogenic [illness caused by medical treatment] complications, are often concealed from the health professional. Frank exploration of these experiences is appropriate. Patients tend to suppress negative revelations lest their future care be jeopardized. Aware of patients' possible hesitancy, professionals should develop thoughtful strategies for accessing patients' histories. Education is imperative. Of concern, is that one survey in a country [New Zealand] with a highly developed health care system suggested that one-third thought that alternative therapies could be used instead of conventional cancer treatments.

Despite the best efforts of well-informed oncologists, sometimes patients and their responsible relatives still

The use of Spirulina herbal supplements, vitamins, ionized water, and other alternative medicines used to treat cancer are highly controversial within the medical community. (© Sheila Terry/Photo Researchers, Inc.)

forego life-saving treatment and follow a mythical and fantastic quest for alternative answers. Unfortunately these quests inevitably and tragically end with widely disseminated cancer, thereby missing the opportunity to cure. Only by communicating within their cultural belief system and compassionately discussing their deepest (mis) beliefs can sensible persuasion be achieved. This approach can allow families to still maintain their belief systems about different approaches, yet still ensure that a child receives the chemotherapy. In fact, many cancer centers offer complementary therapies for supportive care and coping (45% of NCI [National Cancer Institute] designated cancer centers) . . . it's not just about oncologists pushing harsh chemotherapy treatments without regards for their side effects.

Nanoparticles Show Great Promise in Treating Cancer

Ruben Dagda

Ruben Dagda is a research associate and an educator at the University of Pittsburgh and has authored multiple research manuscripts and review articles in the areas of toxicology and neurobiology.

In the following viewpoint Dagda argues that nanoparticles, small particles approximately one-billionth the length of a meter, have a variety of promising applications in detecting and treating cancer. He explains that one technique is to create nanoparticles coated with antibodies or peptides that will stick to tumor cells, then apply infrared radiation that will be absorbed by the nanoparticles and destroy the cancer cells. Another technique involves attaching an antitumor agent like doxorubicin, which is used to treat Hodgkin's lymphoma and leukemia, to a targeted nanoparticle. According to Dagda, research is also being done on multipurpose nanoparticles that can perform various diagnostic and therapeutic functions simultaneously.

SOURCE: Ruben Dagda, "Magnetic Nanoparticles Can Efficiently Locate and Destroy Tumors," Examiner.com, November 14, 2009. Copyright © 2009 by Examiner.com. All rights reserved. Reproduced by permission.

Nanoparticles are characteristically small particles that may consist of one or two elements, about 1 billionth the length of a meter. This extremely small size confers them with amazing physico-chemical properties including enhanced electrical, magnetic and thermal conductivity which otherwise would not exhibit in their elemental form. Nanoparticles come in different sizes and shapes. Nanoparticles can be synthesized with a size range of 10 nanometers up to 100 nanometers (one tenth the size of a viral particle) and with a spherical, octahedral, or cylindrical shapes.

Both carbon and metallic based nanoparticles have a high potential for different biomedical applications including the dual diagnosis and treatment of tumors, hence the term "therasnostic" to describe the dual therapeutic and diagnostic properties of these particles. While carbon nanoparticles have the ability to absorb infrared and visible light at many wavelengths, magnetic nanoparticles can absorb and emit many different types of low magnetic radiation depending on the major and trace metals that make up the metallic core of the particle. Investigators believe that they are ideal candidate molecules for destroying tumors by using a new technique termed thermal mediated ablation due to their ability to absorb infrared radiation, and extremely small size. One obvious advantage of using thermally conductive nanoparticles to combat brain cancer is the fact that these particles are so small [that they] can cross the blood brain barrier with ease via an intravenous infusion of resuspended nanoparticles.

Functionalizing Nanoparticles for Enhanced Anticancer Activity

The functionalization of nanoparticles allows the generation of hundreds of different versions of magnetic nanoparticles that can be tailored according to the needs of a patient. Carbon and magenitc nanoparticles can be

In this illustration blue nanoparticles with cytotoxic drugs attached (shown in purple) target a tumor cell for destruction. (© Medi-mation Ltd/ Photo Researchers, Inc.)

"functionalized" by attaching different biological modules with different functions at the surface of these particles which include but are not limited to: 1) homing devices to target and locate tumors (i.e., antibodies and peptides), 2) drugs to destroy a tumor cell once it reaches its target, 3) special outer biologically compatible coats (cloaking coats) to minimize the toxicity of these particles and avoid an unwanted immune response and 4) a second outer layer that can act as a detonating device to send a pulse of radiation to the tumor cell.

Like magnetic nanoparticles, colloidal gold particles can also be functionalized with certain small peptide antibodies or with an RGD peptide (binds to integrins of tumors) to help locate and attach to tumors. In addition, these colloidal gold particles can be "armed" with antitumor agents such as methotrexate, doxorubicin [commonly used to treat Hodgkin's lymphoma] in addition to other drugs that are released once they attach to tumors.

70

Once the right prototype of multifunctionalized nanoparticle is tailored to combat a specific type of cancer, a patient can be intravenously injected with a suspension of the nanoparticles. The magnetic nanoparticles emit a strong magnetic signal that is detected by an MRI [magnetic resonance imaging] machine which detects the distribution of the particles without the need to use a contrast dye. Once absorbed by the tumors, the exact coordinates of the location of the tumor at the affected site are identified and keyed onto a computer interface connected to an MRI machine where a pulse of infrared radiation "stirs" or excites the gold particle, increases their Brownian motion (vibrational) and emits heat inside the tumor while sparing healthy tissue. This technique works very well because tumor cells are more sensitive to temperature increases while non-cancerous, healthy tissue are spared from the ravaging thermal radiation. In other words, tumors can be cooked or microwaved to death using thermal mediated ablation by employing magnetic nanoparticles.

FAST FACT

The *International Journal of Nanomedicine* reported in 2010 that silver nanoparticles killed Dalton's lymphoma cells in mouse tumors by inducing apoptosis (programmed cell death), increasing survival time by 50 percent.

Multipurpose Nanoparticles

The most enhanced version of nanoparticles are multipurpose prototypes that can diagnose, monitor, and treat the tumor all at once. The idea behind the concept of functionalizing nanoparticles is modeled from coronoviruses and the Influenza viruses which have multiple functional groups attached to the viral protein coats.

For instance, Ravi S. Kane, professor of chemical and biological engineering, and his team at Rensselaer Polytechnic Institute, is one of the first pioneers for using magnetic nanoparticles for locating and destroying tumors at the same time by delivering a deadly payload of free radicals. Their highly innovative technique in which nanoparticles carry a homing device (i.e., antibody or small peptide) locates and targets a tumor, and are coated with different biologically active layers that respond to different frequencies of infrared radiation. Once irradiated by a pulse of a specific frequency, the coat outside the carbon nanotubes undergo drastic biochemical changes that allows the release of reactive oxygen species. The release of reactive oxygen species by nanoparticles

Silver Nanoparticles Are Highly Toxic to Dalton's Lymphoma

Results are displayed in relative units, with the vertical axis representing viability of Dalton's lymphoma cells in mouse tumors, and the horizontal axis displaying the amount of silver nanoparticles (nM) used. More silver nanoparticles = less cancer.

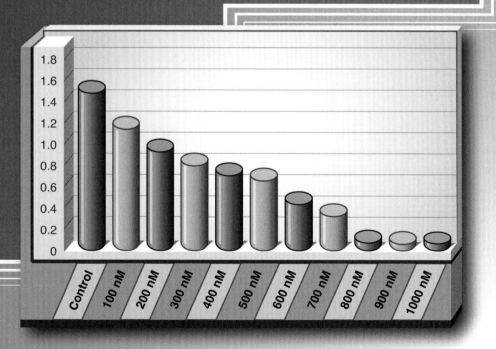

Taken from: Muthu Irulappan Sriram et al. "Antitumor Activity of Silver Nanoparticles in Dalton's Lymphoma Ascites Tumor Model." *International Journal of Nanomedicine*, October 5, 2010. http://www.ncbi.nlm.nih.gov.

promotes the oxidation of DNA, lipids and proteins in tumor cells with detrimental consequences.

The use of thermal mediated ablation of tumors via the use of multifunctional magnetic nanoparticles is a powerful anti-carcinogenic technique that is beginning to gain a lot of attention by the medical oncology community. However, there are several words of caution that have been raised with regards to the potential use of magnetic nanoparticles in patients. The use of ferric oxide nanoparticles can cause significant damage to healthy tissue as the ferric oxide core can generate free radicals in their naked form. In other words, magnetic nanoparticles need to be coated with different biologically active layers in order to neutralize their oxidative capacity. . . .

There are different ongoing clinical trials testing the safety and efficacy of magnetic nanoparticles against many different forms of cancer including glioma (brain cancer), pancreatic and prostate cancer [as well as lymphoma]. . . . Amazingly, these technologies may not only treat patients with cancer at the early stages, but it may be likely that it may cure advanced terminal forms of cancer.

As cancer causes about 13% of all human deaths (just below ischemia), it is clear that magnetic or carbon-based nanoparticles may not only provide hope but may significantly extend the life of patients in the near future.

Nanoparticles Are Toxic and Carcinogenic

Andrew Schneider

Andrew Schneider is senior public health correspondent for AOL News and a two-time Pulitzer Prize winner. He frequently reports on toxic hazards in the environment and consumer products.

In the following viewpoint Schneider argues that despite their great promise in medical treatment for cancer, as well as in many other applications, nanoparticles are highly toxic and carcinogenic. He supports his argument by reporting on research done by molecular biologist Bénédicte Trouiller, who discovered that nano–titanium dioxide, the most commonly used nanomaterial, caused DNA damage that can lead to "all the big killers of man, namely cancer, heart disease, neurological disease and aging." According to Schneider, nanoparticles are so tiny that they can penetrate cells anywhere in the body, ending up in lymph nodes, blood, brain tissue, or anywhere else, where their carcinogenic and other toxic effects may cause unintended harm.

SOURCE: Andrew Schneider, "Amid Nanotech's Dazzling Promise, Health Risks Grow," AOLNews.com, March 24, 2010. Copyright © 2010 by AOL News. All rights reserved. Reproduced by permission.

For almost two years, molecular biologist Bénédicte Trouiller doused the drinking water of scores of lab mice with nano–titanium dioxide, the most common nanomaterial used in consumer products today.

She knew that earlier studies conducted in test tubes and petri dishes had shown the same particle could cause disease. But her tests at a lab at UCLA's [University of California at Los Angeles] School of Public Health were *in vivo*—conducted in living organisms—and thus regarded by some scientists as more relevant in assessing potential human harm.

Halfway through, Trouiller became alarmed: Consuming the nano–titanium dioxide was damaging or destroying the animals' DNA and chromosomes. The biological havoc continued as she repeated the studies again and again. It was a significant finding: The degrees of DNA damage and genetic instability that the 32-year-old investigator documented can be "linked to all the big killers of man, namely cancer, heart disease, neurological disease and aging," says Professor Robert Schiestl, a genetic toxicologist who ran the lab at UCLA's School of Public Health where Trouiller did her research.

Nano–titanium dioxide is so pervasive that the Environmental Working Group says it has calculated that close to 10,000 over-the-counter products use it in one form or another. Other public health specialists put the number even higher. It's "in everything from medicine capsules and nutritional supplements, to food icing and additives, to skin creams, oils and toothpaste," Schiestl says. He adds that at least 2 million pounds of nanosized titanium dioxide are produced and used in the U.S. each year.

Some Nanoparticles Cause Cancer

What's more, the particles Trouiller gave the mice to drink are just one of an endless number of engineered, atom-size structures that have been or can be made. And a number of those nanomaterials have also been

Diseases Associated with Nanoparticles

Diseases linked to nanoparticles from different pathways of exposure.

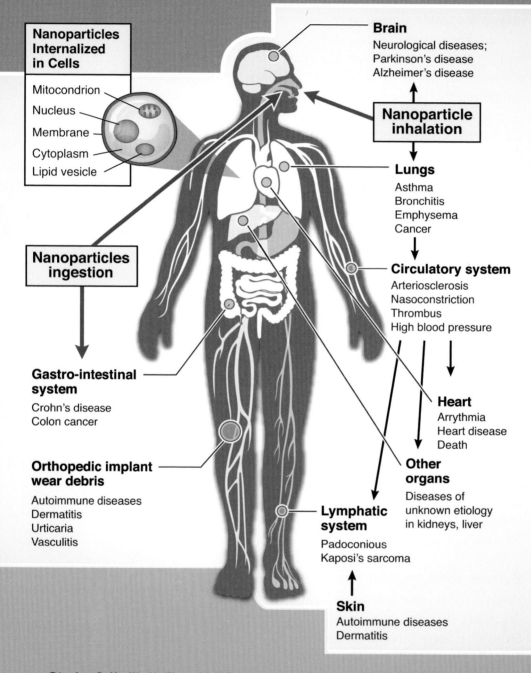

Nanoparticles Internalized in Cells
- Mitocondrion
- Nucleus
- Membrane
- Cytoplasm
- Lipid vesicle

Brain
Neurological diseases;
Parkinson's disease
Alzheimer's disease

Nanoparticle inhalation

Lungs
Asthma
Bronchitis
Emphysema
Cancer

Circulatory system
Arteriosclerosis
Nasoconstriction
Thrombus
High blood pressure

Nanoparticles ingestion

Gastro-intestinal system
Crohn's disease
Colon cancer

Orthopedic implant wear debris
Autoimmune diseases
Dermatitis
Urticaria
Vasculitis

Heart
Arrythmia
Heart disease
Death

Other organs
Diseases of unknown etiology in kidneys, liver

Lymphatic system
Padoconious
Kaposi's sarcoma

Skin
Autoimmune diseases
Dermatitis

Taken from: Dr. Mae-Wan Ho. "Nanotoxicity in Regulatory Vacuum." Institute of Science in Society, October 3, 2010. http://www.i-sis.org.uk.

shown in published, peer-reviewed studies (more than 170 from the National Institute for Occupational Safety and Health alone) to potentially cause harm as well. Researchers have found, for instance, that carbon nanotubes—widely used in many industrial applications—can penetrate the lungs more deeply than asbestos and appear to cause asbestos-like, often-fatal damage more rapidly. Other nanoparticles, especially those composed of metal-chemical combinations, can cause cancer and birth defects; lead to harmful buildups in the circulatory system; and damage the heart, liver and other organs of lab animals.

Yet despite those findings, most federal agencies are doing little to nothing to ensure public safety. Consumers have virtually no way of knowing whether the products they purchase contain nanomaterials, as under current U.S. laws it is completely up to manufacturers what to put on their labels. And hundreds of interviews conducted by AOL News' senior public health correspondent over the past 15 months make it clear that movement in the government's efforts to institute safety rules and regulations for use of nanomaterials is often as flat as the read-out on a snowman's heart monitor.

"How long should the public have to wait before the government takes protective action?" says Jaydee Hanson, senior policy analyst for the Center for Food Safety. "Must the bodies stack up first?"

Nanoparticles' Big Promise Comes with Potential Perils

"Nano" comes from the Greek word for dwarf, though that falls short of conveying the true scale of this new world: Draw a line 1 inch long, and 25 million nanoparticles can fit between its beginning and end.

Apart from the materials' size, everything about nanotechnology is huge. According to the federal government and investment analysts, more than 1,300 U.S. businesses and universities are involved in related research and development. The National Science Foundation says that $60 billion to $70 billion of nano-containing products are sold in this country annually, with the majority going to the energy and electronics industries. . . .

FAST FACT

According to a study from the *Journal of Nanoparticle Research* in 2011, 60 percent of the general public believe nanoparticles pose little or no health risk.

By deconstructing and then reassembling atoms into previously unknown material—the delicate process at the heart of nanotechnology—scientists have achieved medical advancements that even staunch critics admit are miraculous. Think of a medical smart bomb: payloads of cancer-fighting drugs loaded into nanoscale delivery systems and targeted against a specific tumor. . . .

Yet for all the technology's promise and relentless progress, major questions remain about nanomaterials' effects on human health.

A bumper sticker spotted near the sprawling Food and Drug Administration complex in Rockville, Md., puts it well: "Nanotech—wondrous, horrendous, and unknown."

Adds Jim Alwood, nanotechnology coordinator in the Environmental Protection Agency's Office of Pollution Prevention and Toxics: "There is so much uncertainty about the questions of safety. We can't tell you how safe or unsafe nanomaterials are. There is just too much that we don't yet know."

What is known is by turns fascinating and sobering.

Nanopaticles Can Penetrate the Body and Get into the Lymph Nodes

Nanoparticles can heal, but they can also kill. Thanks to their size, researchers have found, they can enter the body by almost every pathway. They can be inhaled, ingested, absorbed through skin and eyes. They can invade the brain through the olfactory nerves in the nose.

After penetrating the body, nanoparticles can enter cells, move from organ to organ and even cross the protective blood-brain barrier. They can also get into the bloodstream, bone marrow, nerves, ovaries, muscles and lymph nodes. . . .

Some nanoparticles can cause a condition called oxidative stress, which can inflame and eventually kill cells. A potential blessing in controlled clinical applications, this ability also carries potentially disastrous consequences.

"Scientists have engineered nanoparticles to target some types of cancer cells, and this is truly wonderful," says Dr. Michael Harbut, director of the Environmental Cancer Initiative at Michigan's Karmanos Cancer Institute. "But until we have sufficient knowledge of, and experience with, this 21st-century version of the surgical scalpel, we run a very real risk of simultaneously destroying healthy cells. . . ."

An illustration shows how nanoparticles can be ingested or inhaled into the brain and the bloodstream. Due to their small size, nanoparticles are able to cross membranes to enter organs and cells. (© Medi-mation Ltd/Photo Researchers, Inc.)

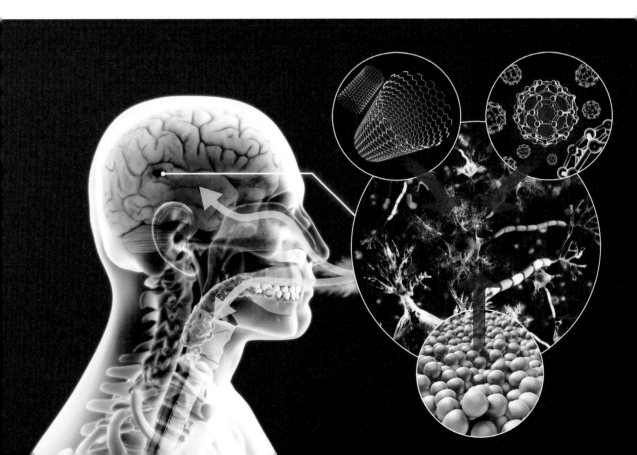

David Hobson, chief scientific officer for international risk assessment firm nanoTox, adds that the questions raised by the growing body of research "are significant enough that we should begin to be concerned. We should not wait until we see visible health effects in humans before we take steps to protect ourselves or to redesign these particles so that they're safer."

Hobson says that when he talks to university and industry nano scientists, he sometimes feels as if he's talking with Marie Curie when she first was playing around with radium.

"It's an exciting advancement they're working with," he says. "But no one even thinks that it could be harmful."

Marijuana Shows Great Promise in Treating Lymphoma, Leukemia, and Other Cancers

Andrew Weil

Andrew Weil has a medical degree from Harvard University and is the founder and director of the Arizona Center for Integrative Medicine. He is the author of numerous books, including *Spontaneous Healing and Why Our Health Matters: A Vision of Medicine That Can Transform Our Future.*

In the following viewpoint Weil argues that cannabis, or marijuana, shows great potential for treating cancers such as lymphoma and leukemia. He claims that marijuana was widely used as a medicine in the nineteenth century, and that despite the suppression of the plant during the twentieth century, there is currently a renaissance of medical research into the therapeutic uses of the plant. The author cites a 1975 study that shows that cannabinoids, the chemical components of cannabis, interfered with the growth of lung cancer cells, as well as subsequent studies showing similar effects against lymphoma and a variety of other cancers.

SOURCE: Andrew Weil, "Medical Marijuana's Tremendous Potential for Curing Ailments," Alternet.org, September 15, 2010. Copyright © 2010 by Alternet.org. All rights reserved. Reproduced by permission.

If an American doctor of the late 19th century stepped into a time warp and emerged in 2010, he would be shocked by the multitude of pharmaceuticals that today's physicians use. But as he pondered this array (and wondered, as I do, whether most are really necessary), he would soon notice an equally surprising omission, and exclaim, "Where's my *Cannabis indica*?"

No wonder—the poor fellow would feel nearly helpless without it. In his day, labor pains, asthma, nervous disorders and even colicky babies were treated with a fluid extract of *Cannabis indica,* also known as "Indian hemp." (*Cannabis* is generally seen as having three species—*sativa, indica* and *ruderalis*—but crossbreeding is common, especially between sativa and indica.) At least 100 scientific papers published in the 19th century backed up such uses.

> **FAST FACT**
>
> The California Environmental Protection Agency in 2009 reported on a study that found a lower risk of non-Hodgkin's lymphoma for both male and female smokers of marijuana.

A Multitude of Medical Uses for Cannabis

Then the Marihuana Tax Act of 1937 made possession or transfer of *Cannabis* illegal in the U.S. except for certain medical and industrial uses, which were heavily taxed. The legislation began a long process of making *Cannabis* use illegal altogether. Many historians have examined this sorry chapter in American legislative history, and the dubious evidence for *Cannabis* addiction and violent behavior used to secure the bill's passage. "Under the Influence: The Disinformation Guide to Drugs" by Preston Peet makes a persuasive case that the Act's real purpose was to quash the hemp industry, making synthetic fibers more valuable for industrialists who owned the patents.

Meanwhile, as a medical doctor and botanist, my aim has always been to filter out the cultural noise surrounding the genus *Cannabis* and see it dispassionately: as a plant with bioactivity in human beings that may have therapeutic value. From this perspective, what can it offer us?

As it turns out, a great deal. Research into possible medical uses of *Cannabis* is enjoying a renaissance. In recent years, studies have shown potential for treating nausea, vomiting, premenstrual syndrome, insomnia, migraines, multiple sclerosis, spinal cord injuries, alcohol abuse, collagen-induced arthritis, asthma, atherosclerosis, bipolar disorder, depression, Huntington's disease, Parkinson's disease, sickle-cell disease, sleep apnea, Alzheimer's disease and anorexia nervosa.

The Role of Cannabis in Cancer Prevention and Treatment

But perhaps most exciting, cannabinoids (chemical constituents of *Cannabis*, the best known being tetrahydrocannabinol or THC) may have a primary role in cancer treatment and prevention. A number of studies have shown that these compounds can inhibit tumor growth in laboratory animal models. In part, this is achieved by inhibiting angiogenesis, the formation of new blood vessels that tumors need in order to grow. What's more, cannabinoids seem to kill tumor cells without affecting

Vials of medical marijuana oil are displayed here. Research has shown that the product is an effective treatment for some cancers and that it alleviates the nausea caused by chemotherapy.
(© Chuck Nacke/Alamy)

surrounding normal cells. If these findings hold true as research progresses, cannabinoids would demonstrate a huge advantage over conventional chemotherapy agents, which too often destroy normal cells as well as cancer cells.

As long ago as 1975, researchers reported that cannabinoids inhibited the growth of a certain type of lung cancer cell in test tubes and in mice. Since then, laboratory studies have shown that cannabinoids have effects against tumor cells from glioblastoma (a deadly type of brain cancer) as well as those from thyroid cancer, leukemia/lymphoma, and skin, uterus, breast, stomach, colorectal, pancreatic and prostate cancers.

So far, the only human test of cannabinoids against cancer was performed in Spain, and was designed to determine if treatment was safe, not whether it was effective. (In studies on humans, such "phase one trials," are focused on establishing the safety of a new drug, as well as the right dosage.) In the Spanish study, reported in 2006, the dose was administered intracranially, directly into the tumors of patients with recurrent brain cancer. The investigation established the safety of the dose and showed that the compound used decreased cell proliferation in at least two of nine patients studied.

More Human Research Is Needed

It is not clear that smoking marijuana achieves blood levels high enough to have these anticancer effects. We need more human research, including well-designed studies to find the best mode of administration.

If you want to learn more about this subject, I recommend an excellent documentary film, "What If Cannabis Cured Cancer," by Len Richmond, which summarizes the remarkable research findings of recent years. Most medical doctors are not aware of this information and its implications for cancer prevention and treatment. The film presents compelling evidence that our current policy on *Cannabis* is counterproductive.

The Effects of Cannabinoids on Certain Cancers

Cannabinoids, which are chemical constituents of marijuana, have been shown to have an effect on certain types of cancers. This table shows the particular impact cannabinoids have on each of several types of cancers.

Tumor type	Effect
Lung carcinoma	Decreased tumor size, less cell proliferation
Giloma	Decreased tumor size, programmed cell death
Thyroid epithelioma	Decreased tumor size, less cell proliferation
Lymphoma/leukemia	Decreased tumor size, programmed cell death
Skin carcinoma	Decreased tumor size, programmed cell death
Uterus carcinoma	Less cell proliferation
Breast carcinoma	Less cell proliferation
Prostate carcinoma	Programmed cell death
Neuroblastoma	Programmed cell death

Taken from: Nathan Seppa. "Not Just a High." *Science News*, June 19, 2010. http://www.sciencenews.org.

Another reliable source of information is the chapter on cannabinoids and cancer in "Integrative Oncology" (Oxford University Press, 2009), a textbook I edited with integrative oncologist Donald I. Abrams, M.D. . . .

After more than 70 years of misinformation about this botanical remedy, I am delighted that we are finally gaining a mature understanding of its immense therapeutic potential.

Marijuana Is Not an Effective Medicine

Drug Free America Foundation

Drug Free America Foundation (DFAF) is a drug prevention and policy organization committed to developing, promoting, and sustaining global strategies, policies, and laws that will reduce illegal drug use, drug addiction, drug-related injury, and death. In the following viewpoint the authors argue that use of marijuana in its crude form (i.e., plant material) is not an appropriate medicine to treat cancer or any other medical condition. They support their claim by pointing out that many national health organizations, such as the American Medical Association and the American Cancer Society, have rejected marijuana for medical use. The authors also state that marijuana contains cancer-causing agents and other harmful chemicals, and claim that use of marijuana has been linked to a variety of harmful effects ranging from respiratory damage to violent behavior, making it unsuitable for use as a medicine.

SOURCE: "Why Crude Marijuana Is Not Medicine," DFAF.org, n.d. Copyright © n.d. by Drug Free America Foundation, Inc. All rights reserved. Reproduced by permission.

The controversial topic of "medical marijuana" is surrounded with confusing and contradicting information. Drug Free America Foundation, Inc. (DFAF) has studied the issue thoroughly and is committed to providing the most accurate information based on scientific and medical evidence. DFAF does not believe that crude marijuana, however, can be used safely as medicine.

Crude marijuana is considered a Schedule 1 drug, the most restrictive designation given by the Controlled Substances Act (CSA) that places all drugs regulated by federal law into one of five schedules. What this means is that marijuana:

- has a high potential for abuse;
- has no currently accepted medical use in treatment in the U.S.;
- lacks the accepted safety for use of the drug under medical supervision;
- cannot be prescribed by a doctor;
- is not sold in a pharmacy; and
- is in the same category as heroin, LSD and Ecstasy (MDMA).

Crude marijuana has been rejected for medicinal use by many prominent national health organizations including the American Medical Association, National Multiple Sclerosis Society, American Glaucoma Society, American Academy of Ophthalmology, American Cancer Society, National Eye Institute, National Institute for Neurological Disorders and Stroke and most importantly the Federal Food and Drug Administration (FDA).

Medications should be determined through scientifically valid research and the well established FDA process—not by the desires of a small group of individuals or the public's vote. The FDA is tasked with determining what is deemed as medicine. That process has been carefully constructed over the past century to protect patient health and safety. All medications, particularly those containing controlled substances, should become available only after having satisfied the rigorous criteria of the FDA approval process. Patients and physicians have the right to insist that prescription medications satisfy modern medical standards for quality, safety and efficacy. Such medications must be standardized by composition and dose and administered in an appropriate and safe delivery system with a reproducible dose.

Marijuana Has No Currently Accepted Medical Use

In *Alliance for Cannabis Therapeutics v. DEA*, 15 F.3d 1131 (D.D.C. 1994), the United States District Court for the District of Columbia accepted the Drug Enforcement Administration's five-part test for determining whether a drug meets "currently accepted medical use." The test requires that:

1. the drug's chemistry must be known and reproducible;
2. there must be adequate safety studies;
3. there must be adequate and well-controlled studies proving efficacy;
4. the drug must be accepted by qualified experts; and
5. the scientific evidence must be widely available.

Applying these criteria to crude marijuana, the court found that the drug had no currently accepted medical use. Preclinical and clinical studies are necessary to provide physicians with adequate information to guide their prescribing decisions. It is quite possible that in the near future we can anticipate that cannabinoid products will undergo clinical trials for their approval, and some may reach the market. There is no reason why medications derived from the cannabis plant should be exempted from the FDA process.

THC Suppresses the Immune System

When mice were injected with THC (tetrahydrocannabinol), the main psychoactive ingredient of marijuana, there was a large and rapid increase in myeloid-derived suppressor cells (MDSC), which have potent immuno-suppressive (immune system–suppressing) properties. In this graph, the vertical axis measures absolute numbers (Abs) of MDSC cells, calculated from an examination of cells extracted from the peritoneum (a membrane lining the cavity of the abdomen and covering the abdominal organs) of mice sixteen hours after the THC was injected.

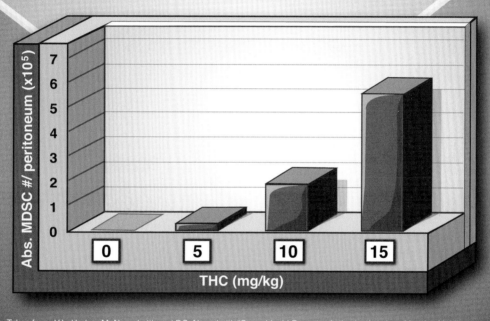

Taken from: V.L. Hedge, M. Nagarkatti. and P.S. Nagarkatti, "Cannabinoid Receptor Activation Leads to Massive Mobilization of Myeloid-derived Suppressor Cells with Potent Immunosuppressive Properties." *European Journal of Immunology*, 2010.

A pill form of the active chemical in marijuana, dronabinol (trade name—Marinol) currently exists and can be helpful for the nausea associated with chemo-therapy or the wasting disease that appears with AIDS. But, even dronabinol is typically a third tier medicine. According to John A. Benson, Jr., M.D. of the Institute of Medicine, research on other cannabinoids is under-way, and some of these chemicals may one day prove

Opponents of medical marijuana say that crude marijuana has no medical treatment properties and that it is a cancer-causing agent. (© blickwinkel/Alamy)

to be useful medicines. However, he states: "While we see a future in the development of chemically defined cannabinoid drugs, we see little future in smoked marijuana as a medicine." No FDA-approved medications are smoked.

Marijuana Has Many Detrimental Health Effects

It is difficult to administer safe, regulated doses of medicines in smoked form. Furthermore, the harmful chemicals and carcinogens that are byproducts of smoking create entirely new health problems. The California Office of Environmental Health Hazard Assessment, after an extensive review of over 30 scientific papers, declared that marijuana smoke causes cancer. The respiratory difficulties associated with marijuana use preclude the inhaled route of administration as a medicine. Smoked marijuana is associated with higher concentrations of tar, carbon monoxide, and carcinogens than even cigarette smoke. Recent studies show the following destructive effects of marijuana use:

- Respiratory damage
- Cardiovascular damage—it can dramatically increase heart rate
- Reproductive damage in men and women
- Immunosuppression
- Paranoia
- Emotional disorders
- Increased risk of schizophrenia and other neuropsychiatric disorders
- Memory loss
- Loss of ability to concentrate
- Increased tolerance to intoxication
- Addiction
- Leads to much higher use of other illegal drugs
- Linked to more violent behavior

Long ago, the scientific and medical community determined that mere anecdotal reports of efficacy are not sufficient to warrant distribution of a product to seriously ill patients. Marijuana is intoxicating, so it's not surprising that sincere people report relief of their symptoms when they smoke it. They may be feeling better—but they are not actually getting better. They may even be getting worse due to the detrimental effects of marijuana.

Legalization advocates would have the public and policy makers incorrectly believe that marijuana is the only treatment alternative for masses of cancer sufferers who are going untreated for the nausea associated with chemotherapy, and for all those who suffer from glaucoma, multiple sclerosis, and other ailments. However, numerous effective medications are currently available for these conditions. According to Dr. Eric Voth, a Fellow

FAST FACT

According to a 2009 report in *Chemical Research in Toxicology*, marijuana smoke contains 50 percent more of certain carcinogens than tobacco smoke.

of the American College of Physicians, some alleged uses for marijuana are to treat the nausea associated with chemotherapy or to create appetite stimulation in persons with AIDS, but there are better and safer FDA approved medications available such as Reglan, Zofran, Decadron, Compazine. Another remotely documented benefit is with spasticity for MS [multiple sclerosis] sufferers, but there are also better medicines available such as Baclofen, Amrix, Flexeril, Clonazepam, Robaxin and Neurontin.

Drs. Eric Voth and Richard Schwartz, experts on marijuana, having extensively reviewed available therapies for chemotherapy-associated nausea, glaucoma, multiple sclerosis, and appetite stimulation, determined that no compelling need exists to make crude marijuana available as a medicine for physicians to prescribe. They concluded that the most appropriate direction for research is to investigate specific cannabinoids or synthetic analogs rather than pursuing the smoking of marijuana, echoing the conclusion of the Institute of Medicine.

A Healthy Lifestyle Is the Best Strategy for Beating Cancer

David Servan-Schreiber

David Servan-Schreiber is a physician, neuroscience researcher, a founding member of the US branch of Doctors Without Borders, and the author of the best-selling book *Anticancer: A New Way of Life*.

In the following viewpoint Servan-Schreiber argues that healthy lifestyle choices such as eating a healthier diet and increasing physical activity can significantly reduce one's chance of developing cancer, as well as help one recover from cancer and reduce the likelihood that cancer will return. He says such practices have been very helpful in his own recovery from cancer and also notes a variety of research findings that support his argument.

At age 31, my life took a sudden turn. I was an ambitious physician and neuroscience researcher who reveled in discovery and glittering science projects. Then, slipping into a brain scanner one evening in place of a subject who hadn't shown up, I was suddenly

SOURCE: David Servan-Schreiber, "We Can All Fight Cancer Better," *Huffington Post* online, February 20, 2010. HuffingtonPost .com. Copyright © 2010 by Huffington Post. All rights reserved. Reproduced by permission.

stripped of my white-coat status and thrown into the gray world of patients: That evening, I discovered that I had brain cancer.

Being a physician and scientist is no protection from getting cancer. But it allowed me to dig deeply into the medical and scientific literature to find out everything I could do to help my body resist the disease most efficiently and try to beat the median survival of a few years.

The first thing I learned is that we all carry cancer cells in us. But I also learned we all have natural defenses that generally prevent these cells from turning into an aggressive disease. These include our immune system, the part of our biology that controls and reduces inflammation, and the foods that reduce the growth of new blood vessels needed by developing tumors.

In the West, one out of three people will develop cancer. But two-thirds will not. For these people, their natural defenses will have kept cancer at bay. I understood it would be essential for me to learn how to strengthen these defenses.

FAST FACT

A 2010 Mayo Clinic study found that non-Hodgkin's lymphoma (NHL) patients who smoked, drank alcohol, or were overweight had a significantly higher chance of dying from NHL than patients without those risk factors.

Cancer Is Not a Genetic Lottery

My own disease is just one case in a cancer epidemic plaguing western societies. Cancer rates have been climbing steadily in the US since 1940. This is not due simply to the increased use of screening tests or the aging of our population: cancer has been rising in children and adolescents at a rate of 1 to 1.5 percent per year in the past 25 years. And cancers that have no screening test (lymphomas, pancreatic and testicular cancers, for example) have been increasing as fast or faster than those that do (breast, colon, prostate).

Asian countries did not experience this rise until recently. Yet, Asian immigrants in the US have the same rates of western cancers as Caucasian Americans after one or two generations.

Thus, cancer is not a genetic lottery. A new model has emerged from the last 10 years of research. It moves away from genetics and squarely into life-style factors that we can learn to control.

A *New England Journal of Medicine* study conducted by the University of Copenhagen showed that people who were adopted at birth had the cancer risk of their adoptive parents rather than that of the parents who gave them their genes. At most, genetic factors contribute 15 percent to our cancer risk. What matters for 85 percent of cancers is what we do—or do not do enough of—with our life.

Life-Style Choices Trump Genes

Indeed, a new Cambridge University study has shown that people who follow simple healthy life-style rules reduce their chances of dying from cardiovascular disease or cancer by roughly a factor of four.

At Ohio State University, another team followed women with breast cancer (stage II) who all had surgery and conventional treatment. Some did not do any more than that, but others participated in an education group focused on better nutrition, more physical activity, and simple relaxation methods such as "progressive muscle relaxation," similar to yoga. Those who learned to change their life-style were 68 percent less likely to die from their cancer in the next 11 years.

Other recent studies—from the University of San Francisco—found that such simple life-style changes in men with prostate cancer completely change the way genes behave, including the genes of cancer cells. This research shows that life-style choices play on our genes like a pianist's fingers play on a keyboard . . . transforming the body's ability to resist cancer growth.

And in 2009 a stunning reversal of groupthink on the role of genes in breast cancer: Women with the ominous BRCA-1 or 2 genes (80 percent chance of developing

Included among the many anticancer foods are cabbage, broccoli, and cauliflower. (© LHB Photo/Alamy)

breast cancer), reduce their risk by 73 percent if they eat a good variety of vegetables and fruits, showed University of Montreal researchers. Are these really "breast cancer genes" then, as they've been touted to be all along? Or are they simply junk-food intolerance genes?

Changing the "Terrain" That Supports Cancer Growth

When it comes to treating cancer, there is no alternative to conventional treatments: surgery, chemotherapy, radiotherapy, immunotherapy or, soon, molecular genetics.

However, these treatments target the tumor much like an army wages war: focusing on destroying the cancerous cells. They do not help prevent the disease if we don't have it, and, if we do, they do not help the body build up its natural resistance to make the treatments work better.

For prevention or better disease management, it is important to change the environment—the "terrain"—that supports the growth of new cancer cells, even if treatment pounds them with targeted attacks.

Modern research suggests that cancer cells grow much faster under three circumstances:

1. When our immune system is weakened and less capable of detecting and destroying budding tumors.
2. When low-grade chronic inflammation in our body supports the multiplication of cells and the invasion of neighboring tissue.
3. When tumors are allowed to develop new blood vessels to expand to a larger size, much like a city expands when allowed to develop new roadways.

When we strengthen our immune system, reduce inflammation and reduce the growth of new blood vessels, we help create an anticancer "terrain."

Anticancer Choices

For better prevention, or better treatment results, nothing can beat the combination of conventional medicine (early screenings, or chemotherapy, surgery, radiotherapy, etc.) with an anticancer way of life: A way of living through which we begin to nourish every aspect of health within our bodies:

1. *Cleaning up our diet*: reducing sugar—which feeds cancer growth and inflammation. Refined sugar is abundant in desserts, soft drinks (one can of Coke contains 12 coffee-size packs of sugar . . .), sauces (Ketchup, ready-made salad dressing, etc.), white flour which is equivalent to sugar as far as the body is concerned (white bread, bagels, muffins, etc.), and reducing pro-inflammatory omega-6 fatty acids (red meats, dairy, corn, sunflower, soybean and safflower oils, and trans-fats).

2. *Adding anticancer foods*: including in our diet every day, three times a day, foods that help fight cancer. Such as anticancer herbs and spices (green tea, turmeric, ginger, thyme, rosemary, mint, basil, sage), omega-3 rich foods (salmon, sardines, mackerel, walnuts, green vegetables), cruciferous vegetables (broccoli, cauliflower, cabbage), garlic, onions and leeks, red berries, plums, blueberries for dessert, dark chocolate (more than 70 percent cocoa), and even a little bit of red wine.

3. *Engaging in physical activity*: it doesn't have to be marathon training, not even jogging. Just rapid walking 30 minutes six times a week already dramatically reduces the chances of a relapse after breast cancer treatment or the risk of advanced prostate cancer. And physical activity has been found to help survival with many different types of cancer.

4. *Managing our response to stress*: we can't avoid stress in our life, but we can learn to respond differently than with clenched teeth, stone-hard back muscles and pressure in our chest. Basic breathing techniques that have been around as part of oriental mental and physical hygiene techniques for thousands of years (Yoga, Chi Gong, mindfulness meditation) can transform our response to stress and strengthen our resistance to disease. And simply reaching out to one or two friends during hard times can even reduce the risk of dying from breast cancer by a factor of four.

5. *Cleaning up our immediate environment*: in-door pollutants, parabens and phthalates in cosmetics, scratched Teflon pans, percholorethylene of dry-cleaning, PVCs and bisphenol A from liquids in contact with hard plastics, radiomagnetic fields of prolonged cell phone exposures are the leading and most easily controlled causes.

Good Life-Style Choices Produce Rapid Improvement

As a physician with cancer, I've discovered that we can all create an anticancer biology for ourselves through the choices we make in our lives. They cannot replace the benefits of surgery, chemotherapy or radiotherapy, and do not have the same support from as many large controlled trials to back them up. However, the life-style changes discussed above are demonstrated to improve health and new scientific evidence suggests they slow down cancer too.

The Effect of Diet on Incidence of Non-Hodgkin's Lymphoma

In a British study of sixty-one thousand individuals over a twelve-year period, larger percentage of eaters of red meat developed non-Hodgkin's lymphoma than did vegetarians or fish eaters.

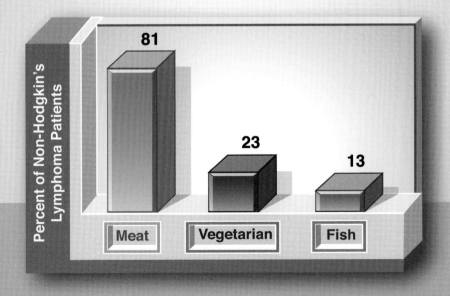

Taken from: T.J. Key et al. "Cancer Incidence in British Vegetarians." *British Journal of Cancer*, 2009.

Indeed, as strange as it may seem, I'm in better health and happier today than before I was ever ill. I feel more at peace, lighter, with more energy and drive and passion for life. A few years ago, my neuro-oncologist unwillingly reminded me of the odds against this happening when he told me "I don't [know] if I should tell you this, but I'm always happy to see you at your follow-up visits, because you're one of the very rare patients I have who is doing well!"

Most people who start on this health journey notice a difference within a few weeks. Recent studies suggest that such life-style changes start improving mood and well-being after two to four months, and can have an impact on cancer statistics within a year or two of follow-up.

What I've learned in my own journey of 17 years with cancer is that the best way to go on living is to nourish life at all levels of my being: through my meals three times a day, through my walks in nature, through the meaning and purpose in my work, through the flow of love in my relationships, and through the protection of our environment. Science told me that this slows down cancer, but, perhaps even more importantly, it brings to my life, every day, a new light and a new purpose.

CHAPTER 3

Personal Experiences with Lymphoma

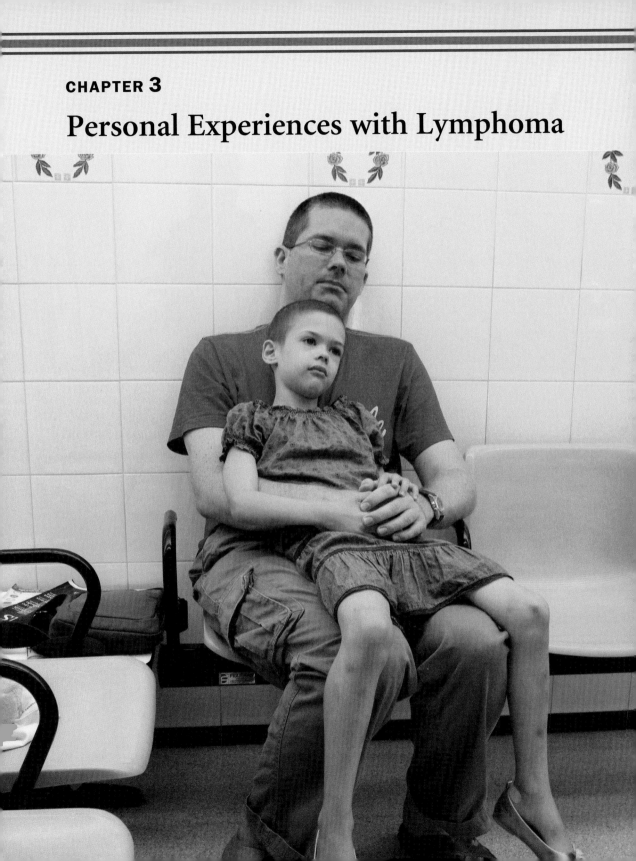

A Daughter Loses Her Mother to Lymphoma

Erika Vogel Hoffman

In the following viewpoint Erika Vogel Hoffman describes how her mother spent the last few years of her life after being diagnosed with lymphoma at age fifty-nine. She also shares the story of her mother's last request to her, how she responded, and what she would do differently if she had it to do over again.

"Erika, go get me a beer!"

I looked at my mom with her bald head, blotchy skin, open pus-filled sores on her lips, and IVs and catheters. "Psst, Erika! Make it a cold one," she added, using her "don't defy me, I'm your mother" voice.

"I can't, Mom. It might interfere with your meds."

She plopped back on her pillow, defeated, and wouldn't look at me.

Mom was dead a few days later.

Photo on previous page. A father holds his daughter as she waits for a radiation therapy session to treat her cancer. (© National Geographic Image Collection/Alamy)

SOURCE: Erika Vogel Hoffman, *Chicken Soup for the Soul: The Cancer Book.* Cos Cob, CT: Chicken Soup for the Soul Publishing, 2009, pp. 240–243. Copyright © 2009 by Chicken Soup for the Soul Publishing. All rights reserved. Reproduced by permission.

Getting the Diagnosis

It's been twenty-two years.

What I remember most from those last days and my mom's battle with lymphoma is that unfilled request.

Mom was a fighter. She always had a "can do" personality, and if anyone could lick something by putting one's mind to it, it was my indomitable mother. But even though she tried, she couldn't lick cancer.

Mom was diagnosed when she was fifty-nine. She finally consented to see a family doctor after finding she had no energy to climb her driveway. He suggested hospitalization and running tests. She pooh-poohed his recommendations.

Within a couple of weeks, I found her lying on the couch with labored breath. I'd brought my infant son up to New Jersey from North Carolina to see Mom. Her neighbor took care of my baby as I drove Mom to the hospital; Dad was out of town on a business trip.

Mom was very weak, and we were initially left languishing in the emergency room waiting area. I told the very passive clerk that I had heard a death rattle as Mom slept. I knew the sound because I'd heard it before when my grandma went into heart failure. The clerk paid me no mind. I called my husband, who was an internist back home in North Carolina.

"Tell the clerk your mother is a GI Bleeder," he advised. "That'll get her seen."

I did just that. Abracadabra. Open Sesame! Those were the magic words!

Mom was wheeled in. Within a couple of days, we knew she had lymphoma. The oncologists were positive that if she would follow a regimen of pills and follow-up spinal taps she'd live another eight to twenty years.

Living with Lymphoma

Mom eventually resumed teaching, which was a stressful job, but she wanted the health insurance coverage and the retirement benefits. A year later, I had another boy and my sister had a girl. Mom enjoyed being a grandma.

Two years later, Mom retired. She spent a year going on sundry trips to Arizona, Costa Rica, and South America. She entertained guests from England and Japan. The final year of her life, my mother accompanied Dad to the Far East for a month long business trip.

Shortly after my third son was born, Mom went into the hospital. Her cancer had returned with a vengeance. She began massive chemotherapy. Her hair fell out in clumps.

I flew up with my infant son. The doc said Mom was not responding. I fled the hospital and secluded myself in my parents' bathroom and howled in the shower.

I called my husband. He began contacting physicians at Duke [University] and U.N.C [University of North Carolina] who might try some experimental drugs to enable Mom to have a bone marrow transplant. Hope again.

Mom was glad to go to Duke, full of sweet memories of her alma mater. She was a Yankee who had fallen in love with the South during her days at Duke. She instilled that love for North Carolina in me.

In the remaining weeks, when the kind physicians tried to get her healthy enough for a bone marrow transplant, I visited Mom each day with my nursing infant. I handed off the babe to Dad in the lobby, while Mom and I sat and talked in her room. She'd look out her door at the hairless children strolling the hallways with their parents.

"I am so lucky I never had to go through what those parents are dealing with," she said with watery eyes. "It's bad enough for an old woman like me to endure this dreadful disease, but it's just cruel for those innocent kids."

FAST FACT

The National Cancer Institute estimates that in 2010, 65,540 people will be diagnosed with non-Hodgkin's lymphoma, and 20,210 people will die of the disease.

Time to Let Go

Days before Mom died, she said, "Erika, I want to die."

"No, Mom. No, you don't want to die. You must work with the physical therapist to get stronger. You'll get better."

She shook her head. "Sweetheart, I want to die. Let me go."

"No, Mom, you have so much more to look forward to."

A tear formed in her eye, and she closed them. I sat there while she napped. When she awoke, she looked around, startled.

"What's wrong, Mom?"

"Oh, I had the best dream. I was a little girl on my grandpa's farm in Pleasantdale."

Mom fell into a coma that night and died a couple of days later. She was buried in Pleasantdale Cemetery, next

Viewpoint author Erika Vogel Hoffman struggled with a request from her dying mother. (© age fotostock/SuperStock)

to her parents, near her grandparents and great aunts, and close by her great-grandparents.

On her stone is written "Be Gentle with yourself. You are a Child of the Universe."

Having cancer gave Mom time to recognize her mortality and to appreciate each day she had, and to live each one to the fullest.

I have regrets. I'm sure most children do when struggling with a parent's illness. One of my biggest is that I didn't listen to Mom when she made a request of me. Instead, I followed the rules. If I were to do it again, and my mommy asked me for a beer on her deathbed, I'd sneak one past the nurses' station for her, and one for me too. We'd sip those cold brews with one hand on a can while our other hands held tightly to each other.

Father and Son Are Both Stricken with Lymphoma

Cynthia Billhartz Gregorian

Cynthia Billhartz Gregorian is a reporter who writes for the *St. Louis Post-Dispatch* in Missouri.

In the following viewpoint Gregorian tells the story of a medical oncologist named Alan Lyss, who found lumps in his neck and was subsequently diagnosed with indolent non-Hodgkin's lymphoma, a slow-growing but incurable cancer. A year later Lyss's son Aaron was diagnosed with primary mediastinal B-cell lymphoma. The father and son battle lymphoma, ultimately becoming healthy enough to complete a triathlon together.

D r. Alan Lyss was shaving one day in May 2007 when his razor skipped over a lump in his neck. He wondered if it was a swollen lymph node, but decided to monitor it for a week. A day or two later, he was taking a stethoscope out of his ear when his finger

SOURCE: Cynthia Billhartz Gregorian, "Father, Son Beat Cancer, Complete Triathlon," *St. Louis Post-Dispatch*, September 3, 2009. Copyright © 2009 by St. Louis Post-Dispatch. All rights reserved. Reproduced by permission.

brushed against two other lumps. They all but confirmed his suspicions. He had lymphoma.

"It was reassuring because I didn't have to figure out too much," Lyss said. He underwent tests and was diagnosed with Indolent Non-Hodgkin's Lymphoma, an incurable yet slow-growing cancer that attacks blood cells that fight germs, viruses, fungi, even cancer. For the next three months, he took a series of chemotherapy drugs every three weeks, as well as oral medications and intravenous infusions of a protein material to stimulate his immune system. Then he underwent two weeks of radiation treatments but the fatigue from them lasted for another two months. He continues taking maintenance therapy which uses an antibody that attaches to residual cancer cells. The doctor says he was tired at times, but never had to stop working. "I felt very lucky, all in all," he said.

Following the conclusion of their lymphoma treatments, Dr. Alan Lyss and his son Aaron participated in triathlon events like this one. (© Hugh Gentry/Reuters/Landov)

More Bad News

Not long after finishing treatments, he set about training for and running two half-marathons to raise money for breast cancer research, including one in February 2008, on his 58th birthday. But several months later, on Dec. 17, Lyss got more bad news. His son Aaron, who turned 28 that very day, had been diagnosed with Primary Mediastinal B-Cell Lymphoma. For weeks, months even, Aaron Lyss had been getting short of breath while swimming. "Then in November, I started coughing and it got bad really quickly," Aaron Lyss said. "Within a few weeks I couldn't sleep at night or lie on my back."

An X-ray revealed an 8-inch mass in his chest. It was blocking major vessels and causing fluid to accumulate around his heart and lungs, compromising his airways. "It was a very aggressive disease," he said. "In the days between my first X-ray and when they first started treating me a week later, the mass in my chest had visibly grown."

Dr. Lyss said that his own bout with cancer wasn't emotional. But Aaron's was. "No one wants to see their child suffer, and cancer in a child is a nightmare," he said. "I was no longer a medical oncologist. I was a parent." Aaron Lyss wore a pump that fed chemotherapy through a port into his chest around the clock, five days at a time. By the last two cycles—there were six in all—he was so weak and tired that he couldn't walk up a flight of stairs or even around his office to talk with co-workers. His appetite was nil. He had to stop running, swimming and lifting weights. During that time, while his mother was visiting, an idea came to him: he'd do a triathlon later in the summer or fall. "The look on her face was, 'You've got to be kidding me,'" he said. "You'd have thought I'd just told her I was going to become an astronaut." In early April [2009], a few weeks after his

> **FAST FACT**
>
> According to an article in the *New York Post,* the earliest known case of cancer was found in a skeleton from 4000 B.C., whose jawbone showed signs of lymphoma.

last chemotherapy, Aaron Lyss began 31/2 weeks of daily radiation treatments.

Doing a Triathalon Together

"Compared to the end of the chemotherapy, that was the best I'd felt in months," he said. "I thought to myself, 'I don't need to wait until later. I think I can do (a triathlon) in a month or two. I feel really good." So he set his sights on the New Town Triathlon in St. Charles [Missouri] on July 19. Then he told his dad. Without skipping a beat—or being asked, for that matter—Dr. Lyss told his son, "Yeah, I'll do it with you." The next day, his brother, Brian, called and said he was going to do the triathlon too. Right away, Aaron Lyss resumed running and swimming several times a week. "But with a different sense of purpose," he said. "About six weeks before the race I bought a bike and started doing two-a-days, either swimming and biking or biking and running. I got into better shape than I was before I was sick." Three months after finishing his grueling chemotherapy treatments, Aaron Lyss completed his first triathlon. He crossed the finish line behind his brother, Brian, and just ahead of his dad, the other cancer survivor. Said the son: "I'm not Lance Armstrong or anything. I didn't do anything anyone else couldn't do. But I was pretty surprised by my dad. I thought he was pretty inspiring. If I can do this at 59. Wow!"

A Woman About to Be Married Finds Herself Battling Hodgkin's Lymphoma

Helen O'Callaghan

Helen O'Callaghan is a reporter in London, England. In the following viewpoint O'Callaghan relates the story of Sinead Gould, a woman in Ireland who was preparing for her wedding when she started having a variety of symptoms such as night sweats, weight loss, loss of appetite, and fatigue. When she noticed lumps in her neck her father convinced her to see a doctor, and subsequently she was diagnosed with advanced Hodgkin's lymphoma. O'Callaghan discusses the myriad difficulties of Gould's battle with lymphoma, including her difficulty coping with the effects of chemotherapy and depression, and how she finally recovered and started a wonderful new life.

SOURCE: Helen O'Callaghan, "I Was Planning My Wedding . . . Suddenly It Was My Funeral; Diagnosed with Cancer Four Months Before Her Big Day, Sinead Walked Down the Aisle—and Gave Birth to the Child Doctors Said Was Impossible; I told Jeff to Find Himself Another Bride. He Laughed," *Daily Mail,* March 16, 2010, p. 27. Copyright © 2010 by Daily Mail (London, England). All rights reserved. Reproduced by permission.

When the consultant told Sinead Gould that she had Hodgkin's Lymphoma, the Navan [Ireland] woman had two questions—would she lose her hair? And could she still get married that September? The answer to the first question was 'yes'; the answer to the second: 'probably not'.

Prior to her summer 2006 cancer diagnosis, Sinead's life was bright. An accountant in a Dublin-based pharmaceutical company, the then 30-year-old was making plans for her wedding. Her fiance, then 31-year-old Jeff Corbett, a retail manager for a fine wine company, had popped the question the summer before. They'd bought their new home together. She'd got her dress, booked the hotel, the flowers, the photographer—everything was set for a September wedding.

But just four months before the big day, Sinead started feeling unwell. Initially, she dismissed her symptoms, never guessing they were clues to a disease that would cancel her wedding, propel her into an early menopause and seriously threaten her chances of ever having a baby.

[Sinead says,] 'I'd been feeling very tired, which I put down to being busy. I'd lost a lot of weight, but everyone says all brides get skinny so I thought this was happening to me. I was having night sweats. I didn't know what they were—I thought it was getting warm, that my duvet was too heavy.'

When she mentioned having small, marble-like lumps in her neck, alarm bells rang for her dad, Rory, who persuaded her to see her GP [general practitioner]. She went the next day, and the equally-concerned GP referred her to a consultant. When she attended her appointment at St James's hospital in Dublin a fortnight later, Sinead recalled other symptoms—loss of appetite ('it'd dawn on me in the evening that I hadn't eaten all day and I wouldn't even feel hungry') and itchy legs at night.

Getting the Biopsy Results

Sinead was kept in overnight and had a biopsy next morning. [Sinead says,] 'I knew it was to see if the lumps were cancerous but I never thought they would be. I associated cancer with older people. I thought you'd feel very unwell if you had it and I didn't. I was tired but I wasn't in pain. Two days later my sister had a baby, so there was great excitement and really I wasn't thinking I was sick at all.' It was only when a concerned Jeff and both her parents, Rory and Marie, accompanied Sinead to get the biopsy results, that she felt her first pangs of worry. [Sinead recalls:] 'We went in and the consultant said: "Sinead, you've got Hodgkin's Lymphoma." She gave me information about the disease and explained what would happen next. She didn't go into much detail. I was in shock and just felt numb. I remember thinking: "OK, well we can't get married in September."' Referred for chemotherapy—to begin the following week—Sinead first underwent scans to see what stage the disease was at. The tests found that she had advanced stage Hodgkin's Lymphoma.

[Sinead says,] 'It was in my lungs, so I had a bone marrow biopsy to see if it was in my bones, too. The biopsy was horrible, one of the worst bits of the whole illness. Thankfully, it wasn't. The type of chemo I had is more effective for advanced Hodgkin's—but it also meant a higher chance my fertility would be affected. Both Jeff and I wanted children but there was no other option, I had to have it.' Immediately post-diagnosis, she and Jeff went to Carlingford for an overnight stay in a B&B [bed and breakfast]. 'We were away but we couldn't get away from what was happening.'

The Debilitating Effects of Chemotherapy

[Sinead remembers:] 'We were sitting in shock, thinking: "What's coming? What's the chemo going to be like?" We were facing into the unknown and it was very hard to talk about the future.' Heading into the first of six cycles of chemotherapy, each lasting eight days with two-week gaps, Sinead clung to what doctors had told her—that Hodgkin's Lymphoma was very curable, that it was their job to cure her.

[She says,] 'My hair soon fell out. That was hard. I had really long hair and I'd never gone to work without having it done. And because I was on steroids, my face became round, like a moon face. To have your appearance change so much, so quickly, and you're not in control of it—that was really hard.' But she was also trying to cope with chemo-induced tiredness.

[Sinead recalls:] 'It was like no other tiredness—if you had to get out of bed and brush your teeth, it seemed like running a marathon. Jeff was amazing through it all. He lived with me every day and saw me getting weaker. He lifted me downstairs when I was too tired to walk and stayed up with me during the night when I was sick.'

When Sinead's night sweats returned, nurses explained the chemo had induced an early menopause. This is a common effect of chemotherapy that leads to infertility in two out of three women. [Sinead recalls,] 'I had all these questions: did this mean I had to go on HRT [hormone replacement therapy]? Would I be able to have children? Would I come out of it? I felt so old. The nurses said it mightn't be permanent, that I had a good chance of coming out of it because I was so young.'

FAST FACT

Hodgkin's lymphoma survival rates have increased from about 40 percent between 1960 and 1963 to almost 88 percent between 1999 and 2006, the Leukemia and Lymphoma Society reported in 2011.

Depression Sets In

Right after she was diagnosed, Sinead had asked her parents to cancel her wedding: 'The doctors had said I wouldn't be able to marry then, that I wouldn't even want to because I wouldn't have hair and I wouldn't be able to go on honeymoon. I knew though that we would get married eventually—that kept me going.' That September—the month that should have seen her walk up the aisle—she was feeling very low, the chemo making her progressively weaker. Two days before what would have been her wedding day, she had to have a blood transfusion. Still with one last round of chemo to go, she, Jeff and her parents marked what had been due to be their special day with a simple lunch in a local restaurant. [She says,] 'I was just so tired—really, I wasn't fit to go anywhere.' She finally finished her treatment in October and spent the next six weeks tired and worried. In mid-December came the amazing good news that the cancer had been zapped. [Sinead continues:] 'When the nurse rang to give me the all clear, I was so relieved—I'd been holding my breath for six months and now I could just breathe again. I got so excited—I could start planning my wedding, go back to work, celebrate with my friends. I bought a blonde full length wig. I'd never been blonde before and I wore it everywhere, all through that Christmas. It was ridiculous—nobody has hair like that—but I loved it.'

Despite her happy Christmas, Sinead was yet to face her toughest battle. Though nurses had warned her, she hadn't really considered the mental toll her cancer could take. Within weeks she had plunged into depression.

> [Sinead recalls:] I felt so sad all the time. I didn't want to get up. I didn't see the point in anything. I didn't see the point in having lunch because afterwards I'd have to have tea and after that I'd have to have breakfast. I went on holidays to Lanzarote [Spain] for a week in March 2007 with my sisters, Yvonne and Naomi, and my mother, Marie, and I fought with my mam [mother]—which I never do.

> I was fighting with my friends. My relationship with Jeff was under huge strain. I kept saying: 'I want to go and live on my own—I want to travel the world.' During chemo, Jeff was able to help me. Now he felt helpless.

> I felt a lot of guilt that I mightn't be able to have children. Jeff said it wasn't the end of the world, that the important thing was I was alive and that if we couldn't have our own, we'd adopt or foster. But I felt terrible— Jeff wouldn't have children even though he was perfectly healthy and it was me who'd had the disease. . . .

Six or seven weeks into this bleak period, one Sunday night Sinead told Jeff that she wanted to be away from him and everyone else. He decided it was time to get professional help. Her doctor diagnosed her with depression, which is common after serious illness. [Sinead says,] 'During chemo, my whole focus had been physical. Now my mind was catching up on what my body had been through.' Antidepressants and psychotherapy got her through it. Some weeks were better than others, but eventually she felt well enough to return to work.

A Joyous Discovery

A year after her initial cancer diagnosis, Sinead once again began planning her wedding. First time around, the couple had invited 200 guests but now they didn't want 'a whole big production', just 25 people in their favourite restaurant. 'I booked it all in half an hour one afternoon,' says Sinead, now 34.

They married in November 2007. [She recalls:] 'On our wedding day, everyone was really aware of how special a day it was because there had been a time when we thought we wouldn't be here.' As Sinead's periods had returned haphazardly, the couple immediately began trying for a baby. A year after her wedding, while on a work trip in Belgium, she made the joyous discovery that she was pregnant. [Sinead says,] 'I'd done lots of pregnancy tests since getting married—I was always hoping—so now I did another one in the hotel bedroom. It was positive. I couldn't believe it. I just started crying and said a prayer. I rang Jeff. It was coming up to our wedding anniversary and I hadn't had time to buy him a present, so I said: "I've got your anniversary present—you have to wait nine months to collect it." He knew straight away what I meant. He was just so happy.' After a problem-free pregnancy, Sinead gave birth to baby Emily eight months ago. [Sinead now says,] 'She's great, lovely, the image of her dad. . . .

'When I was sick everyone told me I was lucky, lucky to be so young and able to fight it, lucky I'd caught it in time, lucky it was Hodgkin's and not another type. That used to make me feel very sorry for myself because I didn't feel lucky at all. Now I see they were right and I was lucky and I'm very grateful for that.'

A Woman Describes Her Reaction to a Lymphoma Diagnosis

Jane Cawthorne

Jane Cawthorne is a professional writer with a masters degree in education from the University of Toronto and is former instructor of women's studies at Mount Royal College. She has worked as a volunteer for numerous nonprofit organizations dedicated to supporting social justice and sexual health.

In the following viewpoint Cawthorne describes her experience of waiting to see a doctor, during which time she witnesses another woman receiving a cancer diagnosis—then it is her turn.

The scene is a waiting room in a busy office used by six doctors, all specialists. I watch the clock, flip through dated magazines and begin to resent this doctor I have never met, this man who thinks his time is more important than mine.

SOURCE: Jane Cawthorne, "My First Minute with Cancer," *The Globe and Mail,* January 8, 2010, p. L6. Copyright © 2010 by The Globe and Mail. All rights reserved. Reproduced by permission.

I check my watch again and think of all the other things I should be doing. I am not alone. The impatience in the room is palpable.

A fortyish woman wearing a track suit emerges from an examination room with a greying, slightly overweight doctor wearing a stethoscope around his neck. They head toward the nurse's desk. His hand is on her shoulder and he guides her gently to the open part of the glass.

FAST FACT

As of January 1, 2008, approximately 166,776 people living in the United States have a history of Hodgkin's lymphoma, and 454,378 have a history of non-Hodgkin's lymphoma.

Everyone looks up in unison to see if it is their turn. The others seem to know this is not their doctor and one by one they return to their magazines and handheld devices, discouraged. I decide this doctor must be the ear, nose and throat specialist I am here to see. Watching him, I try to decide if I will like him, if he will listen to me kindly, attentively or patronizingly.

He begins dictating rapid-fire instructions to the nurse. I overhear snippets and then a request for an urgent MRI [magnetic resonance imaging]. The woman is pale, shaken. She says, "Yes," and then, "I don't know."

And then I realize what I am watching.

Witnessing Someone Else's Medical Drama

I have the terrible sense of being at the scene of an accident, transfixed by the drama, staring. I am back in time, in my 20s, with paramedics pulling me out of a car wreck and passersby staring at me. I try to send them urgent telepathic messages to look away. I don't know if I am still clothed, if I am gruesome. I don't want to be seen like this, a spectacle in shattered glass.

And here is this woman, exposed to me in a way she could never have imagined. She has cancer, and I know it. I don't know another thing about her, but I know this intimate, crushing fact, know it only minutes after she does, know it before she knows what to do with it.

The least I can do is spare her my staring. I pretend to be interested in my magazine.

I decide I like this doctor. He swiftly moves her through her next steps and keeps his hand on her shoulder. "Is there someone we can call to pick you up?" he asks.

And I am in awe of this woman, of how she can stand there and fill out forms without her legs buckling, without crying.

I wonder what she was thinking when she came here. I wonder if she, like me, was mentally cataloguing the contents of the freezer and reading old *Chatelaines* hoping for dinner inspiration.

Maybe she had been worried about returning to her looming e-mail at work. Maybe she was supposed to see her child's teacher today or visit her mother. Maybe she was expecting to leave with a prescription for antibiotics because she had some tenacious infection, like me. This was only supposed to be a minor disruption in an otherwise routine day.

A Sudden Change of Perspective

I think about how plans and freezer contents and work can become suddenly and utterly meaningless. Ashamed of my self-absorption and my petty impatience just a few minutes before, I say a little prayer for her.

And then it is my turn. With a new willingness to wait, I wish the doctor could take a break before he sees me. His day isn't working out too well either. It has to be hard to tell someone such bad news. I promise myself I will make this visit easy for him.

He smiles at me and introduces himself and shakes my hand. I thank him for seeing me.

He is efficient. He has reviewed my tests. He looks in my throat; I say ahhh. He feels my neck. He says something. He waits for me to understand.

I don't understand. Say it again. Something about lymphoma. Please say it again. I'm sorry, please say it again.

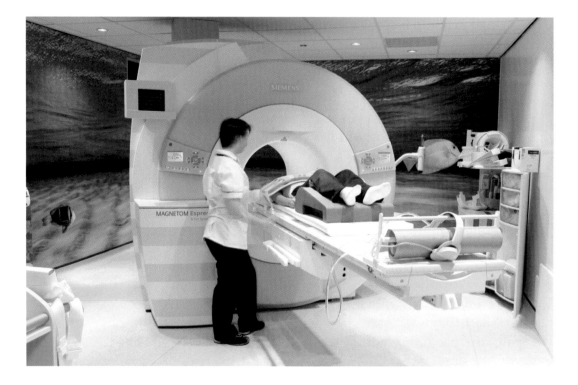

Like Jane Cawthorne, people diagnosed with lymphoma undergo a magnetic resonance imaging scan to pinpoint the affected areas. (© Gustoimages/ Photo Researchers, Inc.)

Then, he guides me to the counter, to the gap in the glass, and dictates instructions. Another urgent MRI. There are forms.

I do not know who is impatiently waiting, watching me, or if they understand what they are witnessing.

My legs do not buckle and I do not sob. I feel the weight of the doctor's hand on my shoulder and the pen in my hand. It anchors me to the present and draws a line to the next minute and the next one and the one after that.

I do exactly what the woman before me did. Without knowing it, she has mentored me through my first minutes as a cancer patient, and I am grateful for her example.

Now, almost six years later, I think of her often and hope that she, like me, is well.

GLOSSARY

aggressive lymphoma — Intermediate- or high-grade lymphoma, which grows faster than indolent lymphomas and tends to produce symptoms more rapidly.

alternative medicine — See **complementary and alternative medicine**.

angiogenesis — The process of developing new blood vessels. Tumors can induce angiogenesis to obtain nutrients for their further growth.

antibody — An immune system protein that recognizes a specific foreign molecule.

antigen — A foreign substance such as a toxin or enzyme that produces an immune system response, particularly the production of antibodies.

apoptosis — Cell death in which the cell uses natural built-in mechanisms to kill itself.

B cell — A lymphocyte, a type of white blood cell that is produced in the bone marrow. B cells detect and bind to antigens. Other immune cells, such as T cells, are then triggered to destroy the antigens.

benign tumor — A noncancerous growth comprised of cells that reproduce uncontrollably but do not spread to other tissues.

biopsy — The removal of a small sample of tissue for examination under a microscope; used for the diagnosis of cancer and to check for infection.

blood cancer — See **hematologic malignancy**.

bone marrow — Tissue inside the bones that produces red and white blood cells.

carcinogen Any substance capable of causing cancer by mutating a cell's DNA.

chemotherapy Treatment with various combinations of chemicals or drugs, particularly for the treatment of cancer.

chronic lymphocytic leukemia (CLL) A manifestation of the same disease process as small lymphocytic lymphoma (SLL), characterized by excess growth of white blood cells. Whereas SLL occurs in the lymph nodes, CLL shows up as cancer cells circulating in the blood.

clinical test The procedure of testing a new drug for safety and effectiveness in treating a particular disease or condition. Clinical tests are carried out under strict controls to assure the most accurate results. The Food and Drug Administration makes its decision to approve a drug or not based on these tests.

complementary and alternative medicine (CAM) Medical practices that fall outside the conventional treatments prescribed by doctors. CAMs are sometimes used in addition to prescribed medicine; for example, to reduce pain or anxiety.

hematologic malignancies Cancers that affect the blood, bone marrow, or lymph glands; types include lymphoma and leukemia.

Hodgkin's disease See **Hodgkin's lymphoma.**

Hodgkin's lymphoma (HL) A cancer of the blood and bone marrow, characterized by abnormal lymphocytes called Reed-Sternberg cells. Formerly known as Hodgkin's disease.

imaging tests Tests that help doctors locate a tumor even if it is deep in the body. These tests include magnetic resonance imaging (MRI) and computed tomography (CT) scans, among others.

immunotherapy A cancer treatment that stimulates substances already produced by the body's immune system to reject and destroy cancerous growths. Monoclonal antibodies and T cell immunotherapy are examples of immunotherapy used to treat lymphoma.

indolent lymphoma A low-grade, often slow-growing lymphoma that can remain stable for long periods of time; usually responds well to treatment but tends to recur.

interferon A potent immune-defense protein produced by viral-infected cells; used as an anticancer and antiviral drug.

interleukins A family of potent immune-defense molecules; used in various medical therapies.

laparotomy A surgical incision of the abdomen. May be used in staging Hodgkin's or non-Hodgkin's lymphoma.

leukapheresis A technique that involves using a machine to remove stem cells from the blood; the cells are frozen and then returned to the patient following treatment that has destroyed the bone marrow.

lymphatic system The vessels, lymph nodes, and organs, including the bone marrow, spleen, and thymus, that produce and carry white blood cells to fight disease.

lymph nodes Small round glands, located throughout the body and containing lymphocytes that remove foreign organisms and debris from the lymphatic fluid.

lymphocytes White blood cells that produce antibodies and other agents for fighting disease.

lymphoma Cancer that begins in the lymph glands of the immune system.

malignant Describes tumor cells that can spread, invade, and destroy other tissues and organs.

metastasis The spread of cancerous cells from one part of the body to another, often through blood or lymphatic vessels.

monoclonal antibody An antibody, generated from a single B cell, that specifically targets a cancer cell; sometimes used to carry radiation, drugs, or other therapeutic agents directly to a tumor.

mutation Changes to DNA (deoxyribonucleic acid) of a cell, caused by mistakes during cell division or damage from environmental agents. Mutations can be harmful, beneficial, or insignificant. Some genetic mutations interfere with the regulation of cell division and can lead to cancer.

non-Hodgkin's lymphoma Cancers of the lymphatic system lacking the Reed-Sternberg cells that characterize Hodgkin's lymphoma.

oncogene A gene that directs cell growth. Altered oncogenes can transform normal cells into cancerous ones.

oncology The branch of medicine that diagnoses and treats cancer.

pathogen A biological agent that causes disease, often cancer. For example, infection with the bacterium *Helicobacter pylori* (*H. pylori*) is associated with increased risk of gastric mucosa–associated lymphoid tissue (MALT) lymphoma.

pathologist A doctor who studies and diagnoses diseases by examining cells and tissues under a microscope.

primary tumor The tumor where the cell mutation and uncontrollable growth begins.

radiation therapy Treatment that uses radiation to kill cancer cells. Radiation therapy can be used in lieu of surgery to destroy a tumor or in conjunction with surgery and chemotherapy. Radiation can be externally applied or taken internally as pellets or liquid.

radiotherapy See **radiation therapy**.

Reed-Sternberg cells Abnormal lymphocytes that are characteristic of Hodgkin's lymphoma.

remission State in which evidence and symptoms of lymphoma have decreased or disappeared. This state may be temporary or permanent.

secondary tumors Tumors that grow after the cancer cells metastasize from the primary tumor. Secondary tumors can appear in any part of the body and do not need to be near the primary tumor.

small lymphocytic lymphoma (SLL) A slow-growing but generally incurable form of non-Hodgkin's lymphoma, which involves excess growth of white blood cells in the lymph nodes. When it presents as cancer cells circulating in the blood it is known as chronic lymphocytic leukemia (CLL).

spleen An organ of the lymphatic system, on the left side of the abdomen near the stomach; it produces and stores lymphocytes, filters the blood, and destroys old blood cells.

staging The use of various diagnostic methods to accurately determine the extent of lymphoma; used to select the appropriate type and amount of treatment and to predict the outcome of treatment.

stem cells Undifferentiated cells found in bone marrow and other tissues that can potentially mature into many different types of cells, helping the body to replenish and repair itself.

stem cell transplantation Injection of stem cells into a patient to replenish bone marrow following high-dose chemotherapy or radiation treatment.

T cell A lymphocyte that can destroy altered or abnormal cells, such as cancer cells or cells infected by viruses. T cells are produced in the bone marrow but mature in the thymus gland.

thymus An organ of the lymphatic system, located behind the breastbone, that produces the T lymphocytes of the immune system.

watchful waiting A treatment option for indolent lymphomas that are not causing symptoms; involves frequent monitoring of the patient but deferral of treatment until the cancer presents uncomfortable symptoms or enters a more treatable stage.

CHRONOLOGY

1666 The first recorded description of Hodgkin's lymphoma (HL) is published in Italian physiologist Marcello Malpighi's paper "De viscerum structura exercitatio anatomica."

1832 Prominent British pathologist Thomas Hodgkin publishes his paper "On Some Morbid Appearances of the Absorbent Glands and Spleen" in *Medico-Chirurgical Transactions*, the journal of the Medical and Chirurgical Society in London, in which he describes what would later come to be called Hodgkin's lymphoma.

1838 A paper on lymphatic disease by pathologist Richard Bright is published, "Observations on Abdominal Tumors and Intumescence, Illustrated by Cases of Disease of the Spleen," in which he briefly alludes to Hodgkin's work.

1856 Physician Samuel Wilks independently describes Hodgkin's lymphoma in his paper "Cases of Lardaceous Diseases and Some Allied Affections."

1865 Wilks discovers Bright's citation of Hodgkin's work. He writes another paper, "Cases of Enlargement of the Lymphatic Glands and Spleen (or, Hodgkin's Disease) with Remarks," in which he credits Hodgkin with the original discovery and names it after him.

1872 German pathologist Theodor Langhans first describes (in German) the microscopic features of Hodgkin's lymphoma.

1878 British pathology professor W.S. Greenfield is the first to describe in English the microscopic features of Hodgkin's lymphoma.

1894 The first mention of chemotherapy to treat lymphoma occurs in William Osler's textbook of medicine, which suggests that "Fowler's solution," a medicine containing arsenic, has some efficacy in treating Hodgkin's lymphoma.

1898 German scientist Carl Sternberg describes in detail the giant multinucleated cells characteristic of Hodgkin's lymphoma, which are later referred to as "Reed-Sternberg cells."

1902 American pathologist Dorothy Reed describes what are later known as Reed-Sternberg cells and creates highly accurate illustrations of them that help establish such cells as central to Hodgkin's lymphoma.

1902 Dermatology professor W.A. Pusey treats lymphadenopathy and Hodgkin's lymphoma with X-rays.

1917 Physicians in World War I discover damage to lymphoid tissue in soldiers who have been poisoned by mustard gas, the first clue that mustard gas or related compounds could be used to treat lymphoma.

1926 Pathologist Herbert Fox confirms through microscopic examination that two of Hodgkin's three cases described in his 1832 paper actually did have Hodgkin's lymphoma. The third had lymphosarcoma, a type of non-Hodgkin's lymphoma (NHL).

1932 Paleontologist Louis Leakey discovers a jawbone from either *Australopithecus* or *Homo erectus* (human ancestors who lived millions of years ago) that showed signs of a tumor. Cancer experts who examine the jawbone suggest the tumor was Burkitt's lymphoma.

1940 Swiss radiologist René Gilbert and American physician C.B. Craft suggest using radiation to treat Hodgkin's lymphoma, reporting a five-year survival rate of 25–35 percent, compared to a 5.8 percent five-year survival rate in untreated patients.

1942 Early in the year Louis S. Goodman and Alfred Gilman, assistant professors at Yale University, begin studying the effects of nitrogen mustard (derived from the mustard gas used as a chemical weapon in World War I) on lymphoma, finding dramatic regression of the disease in mice and rabbits.

1942 On August 25 J.D., a forty-eight-year-old with terminal lymphoma, agrees to be the first patient ever treated with chemotherapy, using nitrogen mustard. Two days later he starts his treatment, which temporarily puts his cancer into remission.

1955 The Institute of Cancer Research begins to preferentially use the alkylating agents chlorambucil and cyclophosamide to treat non-Hodgkin's lymphoma. Although similar to nitrogen mustard, they are taken orally and produce fewer side effects.

1956 Cancer researcher Henry Rappaport establishes the Rappaport classification of lymphoma. He revises his classification system in 1966 and it is widely used until the 1970s.

1962 Physicians Henry Kaplan and Saul Rosenberg of Stanford University start using a combination of chemotherapy and radiation therapy for Hodgkin's lymphoma.

1963 The first combination chemotherapy treatment for advanced Hodgkin's lymphoma is created by National Cancer Institute (NCI) researchers. Called MOPP, it uses a combination of mechlorethamine (nitrogen mustard), oncovin, methotrexate, and prednisone. Shortly thereafter, the MOPP protocol is developed by substituting procarbazine for methotrexate.

1970 Studies show that MOPP is much more effective than single-agent chemotherapy, achieving remission rates of 80 percent for advanced Hodgkin's lymphoma patients.

1971 President Richard M. Nixon signs the National Cancer Act, which establishes a national program to find a cure for cancer. Around the same time Nixon announces his "War Against Cancer" and gives the National Cancer Institute a $200 million budget.

1971 The Ann Arbor Staging System for Hodgkin's lymphoma is formulated by a group of lymphoma experts meeting in Ann Arbor, Michigan. Over time it is applied to non-Hodgkin's lymphoma as well and becomes the most popular staging system for both types of lymphoma.

1975 Researchers at Milan Cancer Institute introduce ABVD, a new four-drug combination to treat advanced Hodgkin's lymphoma. Over time it becomes the preferred treatment for HL.

1976 NCI researchers introduce a new combination therapy called CHOP to treat aggressive non-Hodgkin's lymphomas.

1978 Kiel classification of lymphoma is proposed by Karl Lennert from Kiel University in Germany and becomes popular in Europe.

1980s For relapsed HL and NHL patients, a new treatment is developed in which they are given very high doses of chemotherapy combined with bone marrow transplants or reinfusion of peripheral blood stem cells.

1980 The first attempt is made to treat lymphoma using a monoclonal antibody, although it fails to produce a significant response.

1982 NCI introduces the term "non-Hodgkin's lymphoma" and creates a classification system called the Working Formulation, which divides lymphomas into low-, intermediate- and high-grade, with ten subgroups.

1994 The International Lymphoma Study Group proposes a new classification system for lymphoma called the Revised European-American Lymphoma Classification (REAL). In this system each type of lymphoma is considered a distinct disease, classified according to cell origin.

1995 The European Association of Pathologists and the Society for Hematopathology start to work on a classification of hematologic (blood-based) malignancies, including lymphoma, for the World Health Organization (WHO).

1997 The Food and Drug Administration approves the use of rituximab to treat relapsed low-grade or follicular (indolent) NHL; it is the first monoclonal antibody approved to treat cancer in the United States.

2001 The WHO classification of lymphomas (and related diseases) is published. An update of the REAL classification with minor changes, it becomes the international standard. Classification of lymphomas is based on the growth pattern, appearance, and genetic features of the cancerous cells.

2005 According to the latest NCI statistics, the incidence of non-Hodgkin's lymphoma has increased 79 percent since 1975.

2008 The WHO refines and updates its classification system for lymphomas.

2009 The California Environmental Protection Agency reports on a study that found a slightly lower risk of non-Hodgkin's lymphoma for both male and female smokers of marijuana.

2010 A Mayo Clinic study finds that non-Hodgkin's lymphoma (NHL) patients who smoke, drink alcohol, or are overweight have a significantly higher chance of dying from NHL than patients without those risk factors.

2010 The NCI budget reaches $5.3 billion/year.

2011 The Leukemia and Lymphoma Society reports that Hodgkin's lymphoma five-year survival rates have increased from about 40 percent from 1960 to 1963 to almost 88 percent from 1999 to 2006, and the five-year survival rate for NHL has increased from 31 percent in white patients in 1960 to 69.1 percent for people of all races between 1999 and 2006.

ORGANIZATIONS TO CONTACT

The editors have compiled the following list of organizations concerned with the issues debated in this book. The descriptions are derived from materials provided by the organizations. All have publications or information available for interested readers. The list was compiled on the date of publication of the present volume; the information provided here may change. Be aware that many organizations take several weeks or longer to respond to inquiries, so allow as much time as possible.

American Association for Cancer Research (AACR)
615 Chestnut St., 17th Fl.
Philadelphia, PA 19106-4404
(866) 423-3965 or (215) 440-9300
fax: (215) 440-9313
e-mail: aacr@aacr.org
website: www.aacr.org

Founded in 1907 by doctors and scientists eager to discover a cure for cancer, the AACR has grown into the largest private body focused on cancer research in the world. It publishes several journals, offers workshops and conferences, and helps promote research into cancer. Entering "lymphoma" in the search bar of its website yields hundreds of results.

American Cancer Society (ACS)
250 Williams St. NW, Atlanta, GA 30303
(800) 227-2345
website: www.cancer .org

The ACS is a nationwide community-based health organization dedicated to eliminating cancer as a major health problem by prevention, treatment, and patient care through research, education, advocacy, and service. It is headquartered in Atlanta, Georgia. Its website has a section called Learn About Cancer which has several sections pertaining to lymphoma, and entering "lymphoma" in its search bar will yield thousands of results.

American Institute for Cancer Research (AICR)
1759 R St. NW, Washington, DC 20009
(800) 843-8114
fax: (202) 328-7226
e-mail: aicrweb@aicr.org
website: www.aicr.org

The AICR provides information about cancer prevention, particularly through diet and nutrition. The organization funds research grants and offers a toll-free nutrition hotline and a pen-pal support network. A variety of publications are available, including brochures on diet and exercise, a DVD called "Food for the Fight," and the newsletters *AICR Newsletter, ScienceNow, eNews,* and the *Cancer Research Update*; some publications in Spanish are also available.

American Society of Clinical Oncology (ASCO)
2318 Mill Rd., Ste. 800, Alexandria, VA 22314
(888) 282-2552 or
(571) 483-1300
e-mail: membermail@asco.org
website: www.asco.org

The ASCO is a nonprofit organization founded in 1964. It has the overarching goals of improving cancer care and prevention and ensuring that all patients with cancer receive care of the highest quality. Nearly thiry thousand oncology practitioners belong to ASCO, representing all oncology disciplines (medical, radiological, and surgical) and subspecialties. ASCO creates educational resources for oncology practitioners.

CancerCare, Inc.
275 Seventh Ave., 22nd Fl., New York, NY 10001
(800) 813-4673
fax: (212) 712-8495
e-mail: info@cancercare.org
website: www.cancercare.org

The national nonprofit agency Cancer*Care* offers free support, information, financial assistance, and practical help to people with cancer. Services are provided by oncology social workers and are available in person, over the phone, and through the agency's website. In the lymphoma section, in addition to counseling and support groups, the site offers education workshops (both live and archived), as well as a variety of booklets and fact sheets.

Cancer Support Community
1050 17th St. NW, Ste. 500, Washington, DC 20036
(202) 659-9709 or (888) 793-9355
fax: (202) 974-7999
website: www.thewell nesscornmunity.org

The Cancer Support Community is an international nonprofit dedicated to providing support, education, and hope to people affected by cancer. Services include support groups, counseling, education, and healthy lifestyle programs. Its website offers information on both Hodgkin's and non-Hodgkin's lymphoma, as well as information of general interest to cancer patients and those who care for them. The organization also offers free educational materials such as *Frankly Speaking About Cancer Treatments and Side Effects* and *Cancer Vaccines: Exploring New Approaches to Treatment.*

Centers for Disease Control and Prevention (CDC)
Division of Cancer Prevention and Control
4770 Buford Hwy. NE
MS K-64
Atlanta, GA 30341
(800) 232-4636
e-mail: cdcinfo@cdc .gov
website: www.cdc.gov /CANCER

The CDC is among the nation's leaders in efforts to ease the burden of cancer. Through the Division of Cancer Prevention and Control, the CDC works with national cancer organizations, state health agencies, and other key groups to develop, implement, and promote effective strategies for preventing and controlling cancer. Its website includes a section on lymphoma, with links to further resources.

Foundation for Advancement in Cancer Therapy (F.A.C.T.)
PO Box 1242, Old Chelsea Station, New York, NY 10113
(212) 741-2790
e-mail: info@rethink ingcancer.org
website: www.rethink ingcancer.org

F.A.C.T. distributes information about alternative treatments for cancer that it considers safe and nontoxic. It believes that tumors are symptoms of a gradual breakdown in the balance of body chemistry and that treatments should focus on correcting this imbalance and building up the body's resistance to cancer rather than on destroying the tumors themselves. F.A.C.T. sponsored an educational documentary film, *Rethinking Cancer*, and a companion book to the film. The foundation also publishes the monthly *Rethinking Cancer Newsletter, Cancer Forum Magazine*, a book list, and pamphlets such as *What Is F.A.C.T.?*

Leukemia & Lymphoma Society (LLS)
1311 Mamaroneck Ave., Ste. 310
White Plains, NY 10605
(914) 949-5213
fax: (914) 949-6691
website: www.lls.org

The LLS was founded in 1949. Its mission is to cure Hodgkin's and non-Hodgkin's lymphoma, as well as leukemia and myeloma, and to improve the quality of life of patients and their families. The group's website offers free information and support for those suffering from lymphoma and other blood cancers, including educational materials, live telephone support, family support groups, and online chats. In 2010 LLS invested $72 million in blood cancer research, including $4 million for Hodgkin's lymphoma and $16 million for non-Hodgkin's lymphoma.

Lymphoma Foundation Canada (LFC)
16-1375 Southdown Rd., #236
Mississauga, ON
L5J 2Z1
(905) 822-5135 / toll free: (866) 659-5556
fax: (905) 814-9152
e-mail: info@lymphoma.ca
website: www.lymphoma.ca/

LFC was founded in the year 2000 through the merger of the Lymphoma Research Foundation of Canada and the Canadian Lymphoma Foundation. It provides education and support for individuals with lymphoma and their support network, funds medical research, advocates for the best treatment and care for lymphoma patients, and promotes further research. The organization's website offers a variety of helpful information on lymphoma, including information on patient support groups, webcasts, and a download library.

Lymphoma Research Foundation (LRF)
115 Broadway, Ste. 1301, New York, NY 10006
(212) 349-2910 / toll free: (800) 500-9976
fax: (212) 349-2886
e-mail: LRF@lymphoma.org
website: www.lymphoma.org

The LRF is America's largest nonprofit organization devoted exclusively to funding innovative lymphoma research and providing people with lymphoma and health care professionals with up-to-date information about this type of cancer. LRF's mission is to eradicate lymphoma and serve those touched by lymphoma. Its offerings include fact sheets, webcasts, podcasts, teleconferences, in-person conferences, a helpline, as well as four disease-specific newsletters: *Chronic Lymphocytic Leukemia (CLL)*, *Follicular Lymphoma*, *Mantle Cell Lymphoma*, and *Peripheral T-Cell Lymphoma (PTCL)*, each of which is published twice a year.

Mayo Clinic
13400 E. Shea Blvd.
Scottsdale, AZ 85259
(480) 301-8000
fax: (480) 301-9310
website: www.mayo
clinic.com

The famed Mayo Clinic, with locations in Rochester, Minnesota; Jacksonville, Florida; and Scottsdale/Phoenix, Arizona, is a not-for-profit medical center that diagnoses and treats complex medical problems in every specialty, including a wide variety of cancers. The Mayo Clinic maintains a useful website for the public with hundreds of articles and entries on lymphoma and Hodgkin's lymphoma.

National Cancer Institute (NCI)
NCI Office of Communications and Education, Public Inquiries Office, 6116 Executive Blvd., Ste. 300
Bethesda, MD 20892-8322
(800) 422-6237
e-mail: cancergovstaff @mail.nih.gov
website: www.cancer .gov

The NCI, established under the National Cancer Act of 1937, is the federal government's principal agency for cancer research and training. It expanded in 1971 following President Richard Nixon's declaration of a national "war on cancer." Today it supports a broad range of cancer research and treatment programs. Its website offers extensive information on Hodgkin's and non-Hodgkin's lymphoma, as well as a live help online chat option where one can talk with an NCI cancer information specialist. Publications include *What You Need To Know About Hodgkin's Lymphoma* and *What You Need To Know About Non-Hodgkin's Lymphoma*. Information in Spanish is also available.

National Center for Complementary and Alternative Medicine (NCCAM)
PO Box 7923
Gaithersburg, MD 20898
(888) 644-6226
TTY: (866) 464-3615
(for hearing impaired)
fax: (866) 464-3616
e-mail: info@nccam .nih.gov
website: http://nccam .nih.gov

The NCCAM is the federal government's lead agency for scientific research on the diverse medical and health care systems, practices, and products that are not generally considered part of conventional medicine. Its website provides a wealth of evidence-based information on many different complementary and alternative treatments, and reports in detail on clinical trials that are recruiting volunteers or have been completed. Audio and video material is available on the website, and some information in Spanish is offered.

Office of Cancer Complementary and Alternative Medicine (OCCAM)
National Cancer Institute, NIH
6116 Executive Blvd., Ste. 609
MSC 8339
Bethesda, MD 20892
(301) 435-7980
fax: (301) 480-0075
e-mail: ncioccam1-r@mail.nih.gov
website: www.cancer.gov/cam/

OCCAM is an office of the National Cancer Institute (NCI) in the Division of Cancer Treatment and Diagnosis. OCCAM is responsible for NCI's research agenda in complementary and alternative medicine (CAM) as it relates to cancer prevention, diagnosis, treatment, and symptom management. Offerings by the organization include a call center, an A-to-Z listing of complementary and alternative treatment options, information on research into various CAM treatments, and a brochure called *NCI Best Case Series Program*, which provides an independent and scientifically rigorous review of medical records and medical imaging from patients treated with unconventional cancer therapies.

OncoLink
Abramson Cancer Center of the University of Pennsylvania
3400 Spruce St.
2 Donner
Philadelphia, PA 19104
(215) 349-8895
fax: (215) 349-5445
e-mail: hampshire@uphs.upenn.edu
website: www.oncolink.org

OncoLink was founded in 1994 by University of Pennsylvania cancer specialists with a mission to help cancer patients, families, health care professionals, and the general public get accurate cancer-related information at no charge. Its website provides comprehensive information about lymphoma and other types of cancer, as well as updates on cancer treatments and news about research advances. Also included are podcasts, monthly webchats, and a library with book and video reviews, summaries of cancer-related journal articles, poetry from cancer patients, and other resources.

Patients Against Lymphoma
3774 Buckwampum Rd.
Reigelsville, PA 18077
(610) 346-8419
fax: (801) 409-5736
e-mail: KarlS@ Lymphomation.org
website: www.lymph omation.org/

Patients Against Lymphoma was founded in 2002 by patients and caregivers directly affected by lymphoma. The organization's mission is to provide quality evidence-based information to lymphoma patients and caregivers, to advocate for a health care system that provides all patients with access to the full range of effective treatments, standard and investigational, and for clinical research that is patient-centered. Its website provides a wealth of information on lymphoma and treatment options, a list of support groups, and a list of famous people who have had lymphoma.

Vital Options International
4419 Coldwater Canyon Ave., Ste. I
Studio City, CA 91604-1479
(818) 508-5657
fax: (818) 788-5260
e-mail: info@vital options.org
website: www.vital options.org

Vital Options, founded in 1983, was the first psychosocial and advocacy organization for young adults with cancer. In 1996 it evolved into a cancer communications organization for people of all ages and launched a cancer talk radio show called *The Group Room*. In 2000 Vital Options became an international organization and today works with the patient advocacy and professional oncology community throughout the United States and Europe. Its programs enable patients and their loved ones to interact directly with leading worldwide oncology opinion leaders regarding the latest advances in cancer treatment, research, advocacy, and public policy issues. All Vital Options services are offered without charge.

FOR FURTHER READING

Books

Donald I. Abrams and Andrew Weil, *Integrative Oncology.* Oxford, UK: Oxford University Press, 2009.

Heidi Schultz Adams, *Planet Cancer: The Frequently Bizarre Yet Always Informative Experiences and Thoughts of Your Fellow Natives.* Guilford, CT: Lyons, 2010.

Lisa Bakewell and Karen Bellenir, *Cancer Information for Teens: Health Tips About Cancer Awareness, Prevention, Diagnosis, and Treatment.* 2nd ed. Detroit: Omnigraphics, 2010.

Aditya Bardia and Eric J. Seifter, *Johns Hopkins Medicine Patients' Guide to Lymphoma.* Sudbury, MA: Jones and Bartlett, 2011.

Jeanne Besser, *What to Eat During Cancer Treatment: 100 Great-Tasting, Family-Friendly Recipes to Help You Cope,* Atlanta: American Cancer Society, 2009.

Ellen Clegg, *Chemobrain: How Cancer Therapies Can Affect Your Mind: What Patients, Families, and Doctors Need to Know.* Amherst, NY: Prometheus, 2009.

Peter Holman and Jodi Garrett, *100 Questions & Answers About Lymphoma.* 2nd ed. Sudbury, MA: Jones and Bartlett, 2011.

Marilyn Howell, *Honor Thy Daughter: A Family's Search for Hope and Healing.* Santa Cruz, CA: Multidisciplinary Association for Psychedelic Studies, 2011.

Anne Katz, *Man Cancer Sex,* Pittsburgh, PA: Hygeia Media, 2010.

————, *Woman Cancer Sex,* Pittsburgh, PA: Hygeia Media, 2009.

Andrew Ko, Malin Dollinger, and Ernest H. Rosenbaum, *Everyone's Guide to Cancer Therapy: How Cancer Is Diagnosed, Treated, and Managed Day to Day.* 5th ed. Kansas City, MO: Andrews McMeel, 2008.

Judith McKay and Tamera Schacher, *The Chemotherapy Survival Guide: Everything You Need to Know to Get Through Treatment.* 3rd ed. Oakland, CA: New Harbinger, 2009.

Siddhartha Mukherjee, *The Emperor of All Maladies: A Biography of Cancer.* New York: Scribner, 2010.

Cecil Murphey and Michal Sparks, *When Someone You Love Has Cancer: Comfort and Encouragement for Caregivers and Loved Ones.* Eugene, OR: Harvest House, 2009.

Jamie Reno, *Hope Begins in the Dark.* San Diego: Vital Options, 2008.

Glenn Rockowitz, *Rodeo in Joliet: A Cancer Memoir.* Seattle: Bennett & Hastings, 2011.

David Rosenthal, *The American Cancer Society Complete Guide to Complementary & Alternative Cancer Therapies.* 2nd ed. Chicago: American Cancer Society, 2009.

Kairol Rosenthal, *Everything Changes: The Insider's Guide to Cancer in Your 20s and 30s.* Hoboken, NJ: Wiley, 2009.

Robert Schimmel and Alan Eisenstock, *Cancer on Five Dollars a Day (Chemo Not Included): How Humor Got Me Through the Toughest Journey of My Life.* Cambridge, MA: Da Capo Lifelong, 2008.

Sean Swarner, *Keep Climbing: How I Beat Cancer and Reached the Top of the World.* New York: Atria, 2008.

Periodicals   Betsy Bates, "Young Adults Suffer More Cancer Pain, Distress," *Internal Medicine News,* March 14, 2011. www.internalmedicine news.com/news/oncology-hematology/single-article/young -adults-suffer-more-cancer-pain-distress/004848376f.html.

BBC News, "Gene Switch Makes Tumours Shrink, January 25, 2007. http://news.bbc.co.uk/2/hi/health/6291855.stm.

Sharon Begley et al., "We Fought Cancer—and Cancer Won," *Newsweek,* September 15, 2008.

Biotech Week, "Scripps Research Scientists Find New Way to Attack Cancerous Cells," June 23, 2010.

Maria Cone and *Environmental Health News,* "Doctors Underestimate Environment as Cause for Cancer," *Scientific Ameri-*

can, May 6, 2010. www.scientificamerican.com/article.cfm?id =environment-as-cause-for-cancer.

Betsy de Parry, "HEALTH: Candid Cancer: Victories Are Mounting in the 40-Year War on Cancer," AnnArbor.com, March 18, 2011. www.annarbor.com/health/candid-cancer-a -report-on-the-war-on-cancer-part-ii.

Jim Dwyer, "A Lifesaver Out of Reach for Want of a Profit," *New York Times*, October 18, 2009.

Cassandra Jardine, "Telegraph Christmas Charity Appeal: A Golden Age for Cancer Research," *Telegraph* (London), December 10, 2010. www.telegraph.co.uk/news/telegraphchristmas appeal/8193668/Telegraph-Christmas-Charity-Appeal-a-gold en-age-for-cancer-research.html.

Marina Jimenez, "Brain Infections Linked to Lymphoma Drug Highlight Need for Oversight: Study," *Globe & Mail* (Toronto, ON), May 29, 2009.

James Meikle, "A Kidney Operation Changed Robert's Life. He Got Cancer," *Guardian*, March 22, 2011. www.guardian.co.uk /society/2011/mar/22/kidney-transplant-cancer-robert-law.

Amy Molloy, "The 'Miracle' Kill or Cure," *Sunday Times* (London), February 27, 2011.

Ken Myron, "This New Year's, I'm Celebrating Health," *Globe & Mail* (Toronto, ON), December 31, 2009.

Obesity, Fitness & Wellness Week, "Control of Cancer Cell Pathways Key to Halting Disease Spread, Stanford Study Shows," July 3, 2010.

Erica Rex, "Vaccines Derived from Patients' Tumor Cells Are Individualizing Cancer Treatment," *Scientific American*, June 24, 2010. www.scientificamerican.com/article.cfm?id =individualizing-cancer-treatment.

Jenna Ross, "A Teacher of Life's Lessons: Dying Included," *Minneapolis Star Tribune*, March 9, 2011. www.startribune.com /local/117467513.html.

Natasha Saje, "Down to 'The Wire,'" *New York Times*, April 19, 2009.

Susan Salisbury, "Did Breast Implants Cause Sherry Kellogg's Cancer?" *Palm Beach Post* (West Palm Beach, FL), February 22, 2011.

Nathan Seppa, "Not Just a High: Scientists Test Medicinal Marijuana Against MS, Inflammation and Cancer," *Science* News, June 19, 2010. www.sciencenews.org/view/feature/id/59872 /title/Not_Just_a_high.

John Serba, "Is It Right to Make Jokes About Cancer? LaughFest Explores the Taboo," *Grand Rapids Press*, March 6, 2011. www .mlive.com/entertainment/grand-rapids/index.ssf/2011/03/is _it_right_to_make_jokes_abou.html.

Internet Sources

American Society of Hematology, "New Standards of Care and Novel Treatment Options for Several Forms of Lymphoma Unveiled," December 5, 2010. www.hematology.org/News /2010/6111.aspx.

Cancer Clinical Trials Blog, "Non-Hodgkin Lymphoma: Subtypes," www.cancertrialshelp.org/blog/?page_id=34.

Cancer Research Institute, "New Perspectives on Cancer and the Immune System," March 25, 2011. www.cancerresearch .org/pressroom/2011/03/25/cancer-immunoediting-new -perspectives-on-and-the-immune-system.

David Gorski, "Why Would a Woman Withhold Chemotherapy from Her Child with Lymphoma?" *Respectful Insolence*, July 3, 2008. http://scienceblogs.com/insolence/2008/07/why_ would_a_woman_withhold_chemotherapy.php.

Brandon Keim, "To Survive Cancer, Live with It," *Wired Science*, May 27, 2009. www.wired.com/wiredscience/2009/05 /cancercompromise.

Bruce Mirken, "The Marijuana Cancer Cure Cult," *AlterNet*, January 26, 2010. www.alternet.org/drugs/145159/the_mari juana_cancer_cure_cult.

Steven Novella, "The Hidden Cancer Cure," *Science-Based Medicine*, February 23, 2011. www.sciencebasedmedicine.org /index.php/the-hidden-cancer-cure.

ScienceDaily, "Armed Antibody Triggers Remissions for Hodgkin's Lymphoma," November 5, 2010. www.sciencedaily.com /releases/2010/11/101103171441.htm.

Jonathan Strickland, "The Wide Angle: 10 Ways Nanotechnology Battles Cancer," Discovery Tech. http://dsc.discovery.com/technology/tech-10/nanotech-cancer/nanotech-cancer-tech-10.html.

Suzanne Venker, "Refusing Chemo Isn't Child Abuse, It's Colleen Hauser's Right," Opposing Views, May 26, 2009. www.opposingviews.com/i/refusing-chemo-isn-t-child-abuse-it-s-colleen-hauser-s-right.

INDEX